T0165606

The
Father
Knows Best

When What You Want Is Not What God Wants for You

Dr. Tammara S. Grays

WESTBOW
PRESS
A DIVISION OF THOMAS NELSON

Unless otherwise indicated, all Scripture quotations are taken
from the King James Version of the Holy Bible.

WestBow Press books may be ordered through booksellers or by contacting:

WestBow Press
A Division of Thomas Nelson
1663 Liberty Drive
Bloomington, IN 47403
www.westbowpress.com
1 (866) 928-1240

ISBN: 978-1-4908-1516-9 (sc)
ISBN: 978-1-4908-1515-2 (hc)
ISBN: 978-1-4908-1517-6 (e)

Library of Congress Control Number: 2013920406

Printed in the United States of America.

WestBow Press rev. date: 12/31/2013

ACKNOWLEDGMENTS

To the one true God who promised He would never leave nor forsake me, I am so grateful. Mom and Dad, the evidence of your belief in my ability . . . . Mom, thank you for actively praying for me, especially while I was in my storm. Dad, you have repeatedly articulated your expectations of me. You recently expressed you had not imagined I would grow to accomplish all that I have to date. Your words of wisdom concerning only move forward never in reverse will forever ring in my ears. This book is evidence of my forward progression.

Daniel and Andrew, you will always have my love. I am so thankful God hand selected you as my sons. Depend on Him; you are the seed of the righteous.

To those whom God used to shape/make me, I say thank you. To those who forced me in a place where I had to depend on the Holy Spirit for His guidance . . . it was all for my good.

Dear Reader:

Whether this is an introduction or a reacquaintance with Scripture, *The Father Knows Best* serves as a resource for those facing life's challenges and seeking God's guidance. The text is not just for new converts; it is also for seasoned Christians who are in need of a reminder/refresher of God's promises. It is not denominationally based, but based on Scripture.

When you feel you can not take it (whatever "it" is) another moment, there is hope in God. It does not matter how large or overwhelming your particular situation appears, God is able. My prayer is as you apply God's Word to your challenge, you will receive His divine direction. God is faithful; just stand. He cares, and He has not forgotten you. He will *make a way for you to escape* so you may bare it. For those who do not know which way to go, *The Father Knows Best.*

Dr. Tammara S. Grays

CONTENTS

INTRODUCTION

¹When he was come down from the mountain, great multitudes followed him. ²And, behold, there came a leper and worshipped him, saying, Lord, if thou wilt, thou canst make me clean. ³And Jesus put forth his hand, and touched him, saying, I will; be thou clean. And immediately his leprosy was cleansed. ⁴And Jesus saith unto him, See thou tell no man; but go thy way, shew thyself to the priest, and offer the gift that Moses commanded, for a testimony unto them. ⁵And when Jesus was entered into Capernaum, there came unto him a centurion, beseeching him, ⁶And saying, Lord, my servant lieth at home sick of the palsy, grievously tormented. ⁷And Jesus saith unto him, I will come and heal him. ⁸The centurion answered and said, Lord, I am not worthy that thou shouldest come under my roof: but *speak the word only*, and my servant shall be healed. ⁹For I am a man under authority, having soldiers under me: and I say to this man, Go, and he goeth; and to another, Come, and he cometh; and to my servant, Do this, and he doeth it. *¹⁰When Jesus heard it, he marvelled, and said to them that followed, Verily I say unto you, I have not found so great faith, no, not in Israel.* ¹¹And I say unto you, That many shall come from the east and west, and shall sit down with Abraham, and Isaac, and Jacob, in the kingdom of heaven. ¹²But the children of the kingdom shall be cast out into outer darkness: there shall be weeping and gnashing of teeth.

(Matthew 8:1–12 King James Version (italics added))

Do you believe God's Word as the Centurion believed? If not, what is stopping you from taking God at His Word?

CHAPTER 1

Take God at His Word

Many times we go through life wondering and asking *why* we have to go through what we go through. Another question still floating around is why bad things happen to good people, especially those who serve God. I could answer this simply by stating it is the will of God we, His children, prosper and are in good health, even as our souls prosper. Sometimes events (whether they are good or bad) take place so God's will can manifest in our lives. It is not that we have done anything to deserve what we are facing. The outside stipulation is when we were created, God did give us a will.

God's will is we . . . , but when individuals resist God's will, things happen. Does this please God? No, but He is the ultimate gentleman and is not going to take choice, selection, or option away from anyone. Some events occur because individuals refuse to submit to the will of God. Then there are times we resist submitting to God's will. The question is: are we willing to pay the price for the choices we make?

It may appear people have their own agenda, but God makes compensation for our poor choices. Rhetorical question: do you think your will is stronger than the will of God? No matter what, God's will will come to pass. It may not seem like it is God's will, but do you actually think He did not know you or others would respond this way? It is essential we continually seek Him, so we can receive guidance as circumstances develop. My best example I can give you is Jonah. Do you actually believe God did not know Jonah would disobey, not follow His directives, or not go to Nineveh to tell the people of their sins?

> ¹Now the word of the Lord came unto Jonah the son of Amittai, saying, ²Arise, go to Nineveh, that great city, and cry against it; for their wickedness is come up before me. ³But Jonah rose up to flee unto Tarshish from the presence of the Lord, and went down to Joppa; and he found a ship going to Tarshish: so he paid the fare thereof, and went down into it, to go with them unto Tarshish from the presence of the Lord. ⁴But the Lord sent out a great wind into the sea, and there was a mighty tempest in the sea, so that the ship was like to be broken.
>
> (Jonah 1:1–4)

With this said, we will go into the text. I just received a phone call during which I was rejected for a position I had been seeking; I had strongly desired the job. Keep in mind, I had just prayed again *if* it is what God has for me He give me the placement. Well, the call came a little after noon. The employer reaffirmed how individuals do not like to have others tell us *no* to things we want. He went on to say I should first do additional work in the desired industry then apply again. He also informed me he had applied multiple times before he was accepted into the program he now leads.

Basically, just because it was not *yes* this time, it did not mean I should ignore the possibility. All along, I was thinking, "*How am I to get the experience outside of my current duties, when they refuse to hire me for the position?*" Why am I sharing this with you? Well, God may tell us *yes*, and He may appear to not come through for us, but *all* things (not some) work together for us.

[25]But if we hope for that we see not, then do we with patience wait for it. [26]Likewise the Spirit also helpeth our infirmities: for we know not what we should pray for as we ought: but the Spirit itself maketh intercession for us with groanings which cannot be uttered. [27]And he that searcheth the hearts knoweth what is the mind of the Spirit, because he maketh intercession for the saints according to the will of God. [28]And we know that *all things work together for good to them that love God, to them who are the called according to his purpose.*

(Romans 8:25–28 (italics added))

The bottom line is this: I was wondering why, but it was for a reason. One of the main reasons I wanted the previous position was because there was a substantial bonus tied to the work (something I thought I was worthy of receiving). Well, needless to say, I was going along my way as He would expect me to, and I received another call. The next call was regarding an unexpected compensation. I will let God handle my life; after all, He is so much more capable of handling my life.

Before we go further, let me forewarn you this text is riddled with Scripture. You will notice I use an over abundance of scriptures, because I do not want you to just take my word for it. I want you to know without a doubt what I am saying is backed by the Word of God. Besides, He wants us to remember His Word.

[10]With my whole heart have I sought thee: O let me not wander from thy commandments. [11]*Thy word have I hid in mine heart, that I might not sin against thee.* [12]Blessed art thou, O LORD: teach me thy statutes. [13]With my lips have I declared all the judgments of thy mouth. [14]I have rejoiced in the way of thy testimonies, as much as in all riches. [15]I will meditate in thy precepts, and have respect unto thy ways. [16]I will delight myself in thy statutes: I will not forget thy word.

(Psalm 119:10–16 (italics added))

In the recent past, I often struggled with having the ability to sit down and pick up books in order to read them. I am extremely watchful of what I take into my spirit. I *try the spirit* of a text to see if it is aligned with God's Word, for I know He does not want us deceived.

> [14]That we henceforth *be no more children, tossed to and fro, and carried about with every wind of doctrine, by the sleight of men, and cunning craftiness, whereby they lie in wait to deceive.*
>
> (Ephesians 4:14 (italics added))

One may say it is only a little off topic; I say a *little leaven* will leaven an entire loaf of bread.

> [6]Your glorying is not good. Know ye not that a little leaven leaveneth the whole lump? [7]Purge out therefore the old leaven, that ye may be a new lump, as ye are unleavened. For even Christ our passover is sacrificed for us:
>
> (1 Corinthians 5:6–7)

This thought is also linked to how individuals are so frequently a slight degree off in their teachings. Please know it only takes one degree to miss the mark. Let me give a better illustration. Say you are on a journey to an island; you chart your course, and set sail. Do you know you can miss your destination by charting one degree wrong in longitude or latitude? I say we should read, study, know for ourselves. We are not to go by what someone else says; we are to go by what He has said.

His Word tells us His answers are yes. And if we walk upright, He will do things for us.

> [19]For the Son of God, Jesus Christ, who was preached among you by us, even by me and Silvanus and Timotheus, was not yea and nay, but in him was yea. [20]For *all the promises of God in*

him are yea, and in him Amen, unto the glory of God by us. [21]Now he which stablisheth us with you in Christ, and hath anointed us, is God.

(II Corinthians 1:19–21(italics added))

Also, I Timothy 6:17–19 (italics added) backs this verse with the following:

> [17]Charge them that are rich in this world, that they *be not highminded, nor trust in uncertain riches, but in the living God, who giveth us richly all things to enjoy;* [18]That they do good, that they be rich in good works, ready to distribute, willing to communicate; [19]Laying up in store for themselves a *good foundation against the time to come,* that they may lay hold on eternal life.

Perhaps it may not seem clear at the present time, but He is omniscient and omnipresent (all knowing and everywhere). I do not know if you are like me, but we will just say you are at least some of the time. When I do not understand the reason behind why things happen the way they do, I ponder them and ask God questions about the situation. (Typically, I tell Him I do not understand.)

> [10]For a day in thy courts is better than a thousand. I had rather be a doorkeeper in the house of my God, than to dwell in the tents of wickedness. *[11]For the LORD God is a sun and shield:* the LORD will give grace and glory: *no good thing will he withhold from them that walk uprightly.* [12]O LORD of hosts, *blessed is the man that trusteth in thee.*
>
> (Psalm 84:10–12 (italics added))

I have come to learn we may not understand the reason we do not get what we want, but if we were to see the big picture, we would run to God and thank Him for protecting us from the unseen. His Word tells us the Lord God is our shepherd. We learned this verse as children, but do we still have our child-like faith and believe it?

¹The LORD is my shepherd; *I shall not want.* ²He maketh me to lie down in green pastures: he *leadeth me beside the still waters.* ³He restoreth my soul: he leadeth me in the paths of righteousness for his name's sake. ⁴Yea, though I walk through the valley of the shadow of death, I will fear no evil: for *thou art with me; thy rod and thy staff they comfort me.* ⁵Thou preparest a table before me in the presence of mine enemies: thou anointest my head with oil; my cup runneth over. ⁶*Surely goodness and mercy shall follow me all the days of my life:* and I will dwell in the house of the LORD for ever.

(Psalm 23:1–6 (italics added))

Let God do the leading. I promise He *is more than able to work things out for us* (His servants). He does not need our help in leading us on the path either. We may think we know, but no one knows like Jesus knows. We are to cast our cares upon Him. My brother in Christ, Patrick, preached a sermon on *casting our cares* in which he used the analogy of casting as comparable to shooting baskets.

Let me address *casting all your care upon Him.* To cast is to use careful aim with purpose. (We do not just throw in a haphazard way.) We are to purposefully aim, shoot, and release. More importantly, we do not take our eyes off the goal. Think about a basketball player at a foul line. We are calling foul to the situation.

We are to see our storms like players see the ball. They visualize the ball going through the net. They do not just throw an air ball. They set their stance (stand – hold your critical position in battle). They aim by taking the ball (the situation) visualizing the process. After much practice throughout their lives, they know how to project the ball (their cares) so it will not hit the rim and bounce away. They put it in the air, casting it upward (toward heaven) and they release the ball (their cares).

They see and believe it is going to go through the rim and down through the net. What we do not see is a player micro-managing a ball once it is released. They do not carry the ball through the air, through to the rim, and through the net. They have faith—because they have had a lot of practice—it is gone. It is through the net. Can we do the same with our situations and cares when we cast them on God? Can we stand in faith carefully giving our situation and care to Him? Can we not tell God what to do with our care, how to handle our care, as we cast our care? He has it from here, from the time of release, He's got it. (This does not mean pick it up again.) It is gone!

What kind of soil are you working; are you rock, thorn, or good soil? What do I mean? Refer to Luke 8: 13–15 (italics added), which reads as follows:

> [13]They *on the rock are they, which, when they hear, receive the word with joy;* and these *have no root,* which for a while *believe, and in time of temptation fall away.* [14]And that which fell among thorns are they, which, when they have heard, go forth, and *are choked with cares and riches and pleasures of this life,* and *bring no fruit* to perfection. [15]*But that on the good ground are they, which in an honest and good heart, having heard the word, keep it, and bring forth fruit with patience.*

We must cast our cares on Him, not picking them up again, but giving them fully to Him. I know we may often have difficulty with casting, but the longer we take to let it go, the longer it will take God to fully come into the situation. I can only speak from personal experience, but reflect on it. Are you meddling in God's business (interfering or prying)? Do you doubt? He can do it without our assistance!

> [6]Humble yourselves therefore under the mighty hand of God, that he may exalt you in due time: [7]*Casting all your care upon him; for he careth for you.* [8]Be sober, be vigilant; because your adversary the devil, *as a* roaring lion, *walketh about, seeking whom he may devour:* [9]Whom resist stedfast in the faith, *knowing that the same*

> *afflictions are accomplished in your brethren that are in the world.* [10]But
> the God of all grace, who hath called us unto his eternal glory
> by Christ Jesus, *after that ye have suffered a while, make you perfect,*
> *stablish, strengthen, settle you.*
>
> (I Peter 5:6–10 (italics added))

He just said, after a while He will perfect, set us up, make us
stronger, and settle us. I know God will work it for my good, and
you should believe the same. Life is full of inconsistencies and if
the Word tells us man born of woman (and it does) will experience
problems, than believe it. John 16:33 (italics added) states,

> [33]These things I have spoken unto you, that in me ye might
> have peace. *In the world ye shall have tribulation: but be of good cheer;*
> *I have overcome the world* (italics added).

I just shared I Peter with you, which tells us the adversary is on
the prowl, trying to see who is next. We have to get past the *bed of*
roses view of life. Things will happen, but it is imperative we know
what God says and what He thinks of us. We are special to Him.

> [7]Shew thy marvellous lovingkindness, O thou that *savest by thy*
> *right hand them which put their trust in thee from those that rise up against*
> *them.* [8]Keep me as the *apple of the eye, hide me under the shadow of*
> *thy wings,* [9]From the wicked that oppress me, from my deadly
> enemies, who compass me about.
>
> (Psalm 17: 7–9 (italics added))

Believe the Word of God. He is with you. Hide His Word in your
heart. Psalm 119:11 tells us, *"Thy word have I hid in mine heart, that I*
might not sin against thee." Also, it will assist us as we face trouble . . .
trouble we are destined to overcome each and every time they
arise, just like Jesus did. No, our paths are not going to exemplify
one of perfection and no trials. He tells us the following from His
walk:

⁵Let this mind be in you, which was also in Christ Jesus: ⁶Who, being in the form of God, *thought it not robbery to be equal with God:* ⁷But made himself of no reputation, and took upon him the form of a servant, and was made in the likeness of men:
(Philippians 2:5–7 (italics added))

¹⁷And if children, then heirs; heirs of God, and joint-heirs with Christ; if so be *that we suffer with him,* that we may be *also glorified together.* ¹⁸For I reckon that the *sufferings of this present time* are *not worthy to be compared with the glory which shall be revealed in us.* ¹⁹For the earnest expectation of the creature *waiteth* for the manifestation of the sons of God.
(Romans 8:17–19 (italics added))

Philippians 2:4–5 the Amplified Version (italics and emphasis added) postulates,

⁴Let each of you *esteem and look upon and be concerned for not [merely] his own interests,* but also each for the interests of others. ⁵Let this *same attitude and purpose* and [humble] mind *be in you which was in Christ Jesus:* [Let Him be your example in humility:].

Remember, I warned you I would use an excessive amount of verses in this text. I want you to have the ability to glean knowledge from your reading and to *hide His word,* not my word, *in your heart.* Also, it will assist you as you face the troubles which seem to just arise from nowhere in your life. At this point, I want to ask you a question: are you holding onto troubles from your past? If you answer, *"Yes,"* who is placing those thoughts in your head?

God's Word tells us we, His children, *are more than conquerors . . .* we are victorious.

³⁵Who shall separate us from the love of Christ? shall tribulation, or distress, or persecution, or famine, or nakedness, or peril, or sword? ³⁶As it is written, *For thy sake we are killed all the day long; we*

are accounted as sheep for the slaughter. [37]Nay, in all these things *we are more than conquerors through him that loved us.* [38]*For I am persuaded, that neither death, nor life, nor angels, nor principalities, nor powers, nor things present, nor things to come,* [39]*Nor height, nor depth, nor any other creature, shall be able to separate us from the love of God,* which is in Christ Jesus our Lord.

(Romans 8:35–39 (italics added))

[35]Who shall ever separate us from Christ's love? Shall suffering and affliction and tribulation? Or calamity and distress? Or persecution or hunger or destitution or peril or sword? [36]Even as it is written, For Thy sake we are put to death all the day long; we are regarded and counted as sheep for the slaughter. [37]*Yet amid all these things we are more than conquerors and gain a surpassing victory through Him Who loved us.* [38]*For I am persuaded beyond doubt* (am sure) that neither death nor life, nor angels nor principalities, nor things impending and threatening nor things to come, nor powers, [39]Nor height nor depth, *nor anything else in all creation will be able to separate us from the love of God which is in Christ Jesus our Lord.*

(Romans 8:35–39 – AMP (italics added))

If we are not sure of anything else, we must have the assurance (totally persuaded), we will not let anything or anyone separate us from God's love. Christ settled this for us with I Corinthians 15:57–58 (italics added):

[57]But thanks be to *God, which giveth us the victory through our Lord Jesus Christ.* [58]Therefore, my beloved brethren, *be ye stedfast, unmoveable, always abounding in the work of the Lord,* forasmuch as ye know *that your labour is not in vain* in the Lord.

If our challenges with our past are great, we must remember out of the abundance of the heart the mouth speaks. We should watch the words which spew out our mouths. Also, we must watch what we allow others to say about us.

³³Either *make the tree good, and his fruit good; or else make the tree corrupt, and his fruit corrupt:* for the tree is known by his fruit. ³⁴O generation of vipers, how can ye, being evil, speak good things? for *out of the abundance of the heart the mouth speaketh.* ³⁵*A good man out of the good treasure of the heart bringeth forth good things:* and *an evil man out of the evil treasure bringeth forth evil things.* ³⁶But I say unto you, That every idle word that men shall speak, they shall give account thereof in the day of judgment.

(Matthew 12:33–36 (italics added))

Luke 6: 39–49 (italics added) declares,

³⁹And he spake a parable unto them, *Can the blind lead the blind? shall they not both fall into the ditch?* ⁴⁰The disciple is not above his master: but every one that is perfect shall be as his master. ⁴¹And *why beholdest thou the mote that is in thy brother's eye, but perceivest not the beam that is in thine own eye?* ⁴²Either how canst thou say to thy brother, Brother, let me pull out the mote that is in thine eye, when thou thyself beholdest not the beam that is in thine own eye? Thou hypocrite, *cast out first the beam out of thine own eye, and then shalt thou see clearly to pull out the mote that is in thy brother's eye.* ⁴³*For a good tree bringeth not forth corrupt fruit; neither doth a corrupt tree bring forth good fruit.* ⁴⁴*For every tree is known by his own fruit.* For of thorns men do not gather figs, nor of a bramble bush gather they grapes. ⁴⁵A good man out of the good treasure of his heart bringeth forth that which is good; and an evil man out of the evil treasure of his heart bringeth forth that which is evil: *for of the abundance of the heart his mouth speaketh.* ⁴⁶And why call ye me, Lord, Lord, and do not the things which I say? ⁴⁷Whosoever cometh to me, and heareth my sayings, and doeth them, I will shew you to whom he is like: ⁴⁸He is like a man which built an house, and digged deep, and laid the foundation on a rock: and when the flood arose, the stream beat vehemently upon that house, and could not shake it: for it was founded upon a rock. ⁴⁹But *he that heareth, and doeth not, is like a man that without a foundation built an house upon the earth; against which the stream did beat vehemently, and immediately it fell; and the ruin of that house was great.*

We are to believe what we hear people revealing to us. When individuals demonstrate certain negative or positive characteristics, we are *not* to deny them or ignore them (especially if we have the slightest inkling their motives are not pure). He tells us how to apply what we see, when we observe and know people by their fruit.

> [17]Now I beseech you, brethren, *mark them which cause divisions and offences contrary to the doctrine* which ye have learned; and *avoid them.* [18]For they that are *such serve not our Lord Jesus Christ,* but *their own belly;* and by good words and fair speeches deceive the hearts of the simple.
>
> (Romans 16:17–18 (italics added))

If we want to become more than a conqueror, we must *trust* God, not man. Man will fall short of His promises . . . man will fail us every time, because they are *not* God. God never fails! I like to keep the question of what is the motive in the back of my mind. I am reminded of a story my father would tell about one of his teachers—Miss Sade Thomas—who would walk around and mark a check beside anyone who was misbehaving. Perhaps we should take note from Miss Thomas's example, which is the epitome of the 37th division Psalm.

> [32]*The wicked watcheth the righteous, and seeketh to slay him.* [33]The LORD will not leave him in his hand, nor condemn him when he is judged. [34]*Wait on the LORD, and keep his way, and he shall exalt thee to inherit the land:* when the wicked are cut off, thou shalt see it. [35]I have seen the wicked in great power, and spreading himself like a green bay tree. [36]Yet he passed away, and, lo, he was not: yea, I sought him, but he could not be found. [37]*Mark the perfect man, and behold the upright:* for the end of that man is peace. [38]But *the transgressors shall be destroyed together: the end of the wicked shall be cut off.* [39]But *the salvation of the righteous is of the LORD: he is their strength in the time of trouble.* [40]And the LORD shall help

them, and deliver them: *he shall deliver them from the wicked, and save them,* because they trust in him.

(Psalm 37:32–40 (italics added))

On the other hand, by their fruit we are going to know who is on our side. I have been told I am not to judge. My response is I am not judging, but I have been called to inspect an individual's fruit. Even Jesus cursed the fig tree when it did not produce the proper fruit in due time. We can ignore the hints (sometimes they are not hints but blatant acknowledgements) if we want, but in so doing we will suffer the consequences of our lack of appropriate response.

[13]Enter ye in at the strait gate: *for wide is the gate, and broad is the way, that leadeth to destruction,* and many there be which go in threat: [14]Because *strait is the gate, and narrow is the way, which leadeth unto life,* and few there be that find it. [15]*Beware of false prophets, which come to you in sheep's clothing, but inwardly they are ravening wolves.* [16]Ye shall know them by their fruits. Do men gather grapes of thorns, or figs of thistles? [17]Even so *every good tree bringeth forth good fruit;* but *a corrupt tree bringeth forth evil fruit.* [18]*A good tree cannot bring forth evil fruit, neither can a corrupt tree bring forth good fruit.* [19]Every tree that bringeth not forth good fruit is hewn down, and cast into the fire. [20]Wherefore by their fruits ye shall know them.

(Matthew 7:13–20 (italics added))

The Bible is clear and states through Scripture, some I previously mentioned, *what is in the heart is going to come out* through the mouth. It is like when we put an item in a press, what is in it will come out it. My best example is, I like to cook with fresh garlic. Imagine my surprise if I were to put a garlic clove in the press and a strange aroma were to become emitted from the clove. Well, instantly I would identify the scent as coming from the clove and dispose of it, for it is not good for consumption. The same goes for people.

Stop! I am not saying people are disposable, I am saying step back and evaluate; become more reflective.

When individuals get in the *press*—a heated situation—they are going to let us know who or what is resting and ruling inside them in short order. I am not saying the enemy will raise his head, flash a neon sign, and let us know he is using a particular individual on a continual basis. Remember we just read how he is cunning; he may even leave for a season. We are to know who is using or speaking through people, how he is using his servants. Yes, I said his servants, for who are they? I am saying this in the sense they are doing his bidding, and it is exactly what a servant does. The previous scriptures are plain and tell us a person is either good or evil. The situation may improve for a time, but if they are not *filled* with the Holy Spirit, anything is likely to come out them when they are in our presence.

Speaking of having the Holy Ghost, if we are not operating through the power of the anointing of the Holy Spirit we are like a bandit running around without bullets in their gun. Yes, the appearance of the gun is intimidating, but without ammunition, what good is it? None, whatsoever! Look at what Paul said to the people of Ephesus:

> [1]And it came to pass, that, while Apollos was at Corinth, Paul having passed through the upper coasts came to Ephesus: and finding certain disciples, [2]He said unto them, *Have ye received the Holy Ghost since ye believed?* And they said unto him, We have not so much as heard whether there be any Holy Ghost. [3]And he said unto them, Unto what then were ye baptized? And they said, Unto John's baptism. [4]Then said Paul, John verily baptized with the baptism of repentance, saying unto the people, that they should believe on him which should come after him, that is, on Christ Jesus. [5]When they heard this, *they were baptized in the name of the Lord Jesus.* [6]*And when Paul had laid*

his hands upon them, the Holy Ghost came on them; and they spake with tongues, and prophesied.

(Acts 19:1–6 (italics added))

We have authority through Christ Jesus. (If you did not know you have authority, let me inform you if you are in Christ, and you are one of His, you have *great* authority.)

[4]Ye are of God, little children, and have overcome them: because *greater is he* that *is* in you, *than he that is in the world.*

(I John 4:4 (italics added))

I am not saying the adversary is powerless, but I am saying what is resting and ruling inside us is *greater.* We have to know Satan does not have any new tactics; what he was doing in Biblical times, he is still trying today. I will use the example of one of the disciples to demonstrate what I mean.

[31]And the Lord said, *Simon, Simon, behold, Satan hath desired to have you, that he may sift you as wheat:* [32]*But I have prayed for thee, that thy faith fail not:* and when thou art converted, strengthen thy brethren.

(Luke 22: 31–32 (italics added))

God has made provisions for us. We *must have faith.* Use our faith to *stand strong* in the midst of a storm. While I am on this subject, if we are *converted* we are to make sure we do as the Word instructs and help to strengthen those who are weak. We are not to become a tool of the adversary and buy into and contribute to someone's weakness. Ephesians 6:10–11 (italics added) is a strong scripture on which to lean:

[10]Finally, my brethren, be strong in the Lord, and in the power of his might. [11]*Put on the whole armour of God, that ye may be able to stand against the wiles of the devil.*

15

In 1998, I was asked to deliver a teaching for a women's fellowship. This aforementioned scripture was the basis for the fellowship/ prayer breakfast, and I believe it is well worth sharing again. Earlier, we read about casting our care and standing. Well, standing was basically the premise for *Don't Get Yourself in Trouble*, the theme for the fellowship. There are five areas of focus to keep us from trouble. They are as follows: clean up, lay aside for the fight, put on Jesus, put on your armor, and kill the flesh. These are also the titles of the upcoming chapters, which I have disseminated.

CHAPTER 2

Clean Up

Frequently, people do not want to clean after themselves, and God forbid they should have to clean after someone else. If you have a sibling(s), have a flashback to when you were little. This was one of the main grounds for fussing and arguments you may or may not have lost. Guess what, God has a viewpoint on this matter. He wants us to present ourselves in a certain manner.

> [1]I beseech you therefore, brethren, by the mercies of God, that ye *present your bodies a living sacrifice, holy, acceptable unto God, which is your reasonable service.* [2]And *be not conformed to this world: but be ye transformed by the renewing of your mind,* that ye may prove what is that *good, and acceptable, and perfect, will of God.* [3]For I say, through the grace given unto me, to every man that is among you, *not to think of himself more highly than he ought to think;* but to *think soberly,* according as God *hath dealt to every man the measure of faith.*
>
> (Romans 12:1–3 (italics added))

How do we go about successfully doing this? Well, it is the application of a combination of scriptures.

> [12]*Having damnation* (condemnation), *because they have cast off their first faith* (promises). [13]*And withal they learn to be idle, wandering about from house to house; and not only idle, but tattlers* (gossips) *also and busybodies, speaking things which they ought not.* [14]I will therefore

that the younger women marry, bear children, guide the house, give none occasion to the adversary to speak reproachfully.

(I Timothy 5:12–14 (emphasis and italics added))

Please know the devil wants to get us out the promises of God. Below you will find a small list of some of His promises to us:

o   Love, peace, joy, long life, power
o   God hath not given us the spirit of fear
o   Eternal life
o   Want for nothing

The devil comes to steal, to kill, and to destroy. Jesus—on the other hand—does the opposite.

⁹I am the door: by me if any man enter in, *he shall be saved,* and shall go in and out, and find pasture. *¹⁰The thief cometh not, but for to steal, and to kill, and to destroy:* I am come that they *might have life, and that they might have it more abundantly.* ¹¹I am the good shepherd: the good shepherd *giveth his life for the sheep.*

(John 10:9–11(italics added))

We cause ourselves to suffer or to be damned, when we indulge in areas mentioned in I Timothy 5:12 (see above). God already made provisions for us to the contrary with John 10:9–11. While I am at it, let me share a few areas of focus for clean-up time.

¹⁶These six things *doth the LORD hate* (to reject from fellowship): yea, seven are an *abomination* unto him: *¹⁷A proud look, a lying tongue, and hands that shed innocent blood, ¹⁸An heart that deviseth wicked imaginations, feet that be swift in running to mischief* (to devise wicked plans), *¹⁹A false witness that speaketh lies, and he that soweth discord among brethren.*

(Proverbs 6:16–19 (emphasis and italics added))

Tattling, busybodies, speaking lies and/or things which they ought not, all of these actions sow discord. This is the adversary's job. We know he is the accuser of the brethren, so if we are taking on such a role, what does it say about us? I am just asking. Do not become a partaker of these kinds of conversations. Even when we are frustrated, we must make sure we remember who we belong to and His desire for us. Let God handle it. He will instruct us on what to say and what not to say. We have to make sure we remain obedient to His will, for it is truly better than sacrifice.

> [21]But the people took from the spoil sheep and oxen, the chief of the things to be utterly destroyed, to sacrifice to the Lord your God in Gilgal. [22]Samuel said, Has *the Lord as great a delight in burnt offerings and sacrifices as in obeying the voice of the Lord?* Behold, to obey is better than sacrifice, and to hearken than the fat of rams. [23]For *rebellion is as the sin of witchcraft, and stubbornness is as idolatry* and *teraphim* (household good luck images). Because you have rejected the Word of the Lord, He also has rejected you from being king.
> (1 Samuel 15:21–23 – AMP (emphasis and italics added))

The devil is the accuser, we can not let him trick us into accusing. We have to choose to stay out the acts of the flesh, especially things which go against the will of God.

> [6]But he giveth more grace. Wherefore he saith, *God resisteth the proud, but giveth grace unto the humble.* [7]*Submit* yourselves therefore to God. *Resist the devil, and he will flee from you.* [8]Draw nigh to God, and he will draw nigh to you. *Cleanse your hands,* ye sinners; and *purify your hearts,* ye double minded.
> (James 4:6–8 (italics added))

The key is to stay out the flesh. You may ask how does one stay out the flesh? Well, the following are some tips from Romans 8:

> [1]There is therefore now *no condemnation* to them which are in Christ Jesus, *who walk not after the flesh, but after the Spirit.* [2]For

the law of the Spirit of life in Christ Jesus hath made me *free from the law of sin and death.* ³For what the law could not do, in that it was weak through the flesh, God sending his own Son in the likeness of sinful flesh, and for sin, *condemned sin in the flesh:* ⁴That the *righteousness of the law might be fulfilled in us, who walk not after the flesh, but after the Spirit.* ⁵For *they that are after the flesh do mind the things of the flesh;* but they that are *after the Spirit the things of the Spirit.* ⁶For *to be carnally minded is death;* but to be *spiritually minded is life and peace.* ⁷Because the *carnal mind is enmity against God:* for it is not subject to the law of God, neither indeed can be. ⁸So then *they that are in the flesh cannot please God.* ⁹But *ye are not in the flesh, but in the Spirit,* if so be that the *Spirit of God dwell in you.* Now *if any man have not the Spirit of Christ, he is none of his.* ¹⁰And *if Christ be in you, the body is dead because of sin;* but *the Spirit is life because of righteousness.* ¹¹But *if* the Spirit of him that raised up Jesus from the dead *dwell in you,* he that raised up Christ from the dead shall also *quicken your mortal bodies by his Spirit that dwelleth in you.* ¹²Therefore, brethren, we are debtors, not to the flesh, to live after the flesh. ¹³For if ye live after the flesh, ye shall die: but *if ye through the Spirit do mortify the deeds of the body, ye shall live.* ¹⁴*For as many as are led by the Spirit of God, they are the sons of God.* ¹⁵*For ye have not received the spirit of bondage again to fear; but ye have received the Spirit of adoption, whereby we cry, Abba, Father.*

(Romans 8:1–15 (italics added))

It is our choice. God is not ever going to insist we do things His way. My uncle would say it like this, "I can't make you do anything, but I can sure make you wish you did." Do not go through life with unnecessary preventable regrets . . . wishing you had listened the first time to the instruction of God. We can have damnation *(condemnation)* as stated in I Timothy 5:12–14; or we can have Romans 8:1–15 *(none)*. The devil wants to condemn us, but this is what he has been known for since the beginning of time. Put God's Word on him. It is imperative we learn to *pray* the *Word* of God. It is the only way we can put the adversary in his place, and whatever we do, we can not submit to the ploy of the devil. We are told to resist the devil.

We have been made free from the law of sin and death, if He is our Father. He truly wants us in right standing *(righteousness)* walking in the Spirit. Look at verse four above. I ask the question, if we are not walking in the Spirit, then what is operating? Look at Romans 8 again and then you tell me. Are we minding the things of the flesh, or the things of the Spirit? Verse seven uses carnally minded when talking about operating in the flesh. He then tells us the carnal mind is enmity against God. Enmity is interpreted as an enemy, antagonistic, or hostile. If we are in the flesh we are acting carnal and we are not pleasing God. So later, the passage tells us if we do not have the Spirit of God in us, we are not His. He actually said if the Spirit does dwell in us, we are His son and He is our Father. If we do not belong, we will have to prepare to hear *depart from me,* because it is the same Spirit which is required for quickening *(accelerating or speeding up).*

We are still talking about cleaning up, so I want to remain mindful and ask *how can we* stay out the flesh, when we continuously associate with fleshly individuals? He tells us to stay away from these kinds of individuals.

> [17]Now I beseech you, brethren, *mark them which cause divisions and offences contrary to the doctrine which ye have learned; and avoid them.* [18]For they that are *such serve not our Lord Jesus Christ, but their own belly;* and by good words and fair speeches *deceive the hearts of the simple.*
>
> (Romans 16:17–18 (italics added))

We need to do inventory on friends, associates *(clean out, mark, or check)*. Are they worth not being called a son? I will answer absolutely not. No, they are not. No one is worth our salvation. We can not parish because we fail to sever ties and cut someone

21

loose. His Word continuously warns us telling us to avoid, to shun, and to watch for these individuals. Let me prove it by presenting Matthew 12:35–37 (italics added) again.

> *[35]A good man out of the good treasure of the heart bringeth forth good things: and an evil man out of the evil treasure bringeth forth evil things.* [36]But I say unto you, That *every idle word* that men shall speak, they *shall give account thereof in the day of judgment.* [37]For *by thy words thou shalt be justified, and by thy words thou shalt be condemned.*

It is time out for justifying certain traits. How many times have we heard someone say, *"Oh, that's just how __(fill in the blank__ is; that's just their personality."* No more excuses; it is time to choose. No condemnation! Basically, we can not keep doing wrong and acting insensitive to Jesus and the call He has placed on our lives. A person can not repeatedly do evil and not become considered evil. There is hope in Christ, because through Him we are made new creatures. When I said it is time, it is high time to decide and stop acting slothful about what we are to do.

> *[10]Love worketh no ill to his neighbour:* therefore love is the fulfilling of the law. [11]And that, knowing the time, that now *it is high time to awake out of sleep: for now is our salvation nearer than when we believed.*
>
> (Romans 13:10–11 (italics added))

Please do not think the adversary will let us get by in this area; he will try us if this is or has the potential to become a part of our lives. Why . . . , because he is the accuser of the brethren. He is on the prowl. Does this sound familiar from earlier?

> *[7]Casting all your care upon him; for he careth for you. [8]Be sober, be vigilant; because your adversary the devil, as a roaring lion, walketh about, seeking whom he may devour:* [9]Whom resist stedfast in the

faith, knowing that the same afflictions are accomplished in your brethren that are in the world.

(1 Peter 5:7–9 (italics added))

¹⁰And I heard a loud voice saying in heaven, Now is come salvation, and strength, and the kingdom of our God, and the power of his Christ: for the *accuser of our brethren is cast down,* which *accused them before our God day and night.*

(Revelation 12:10 (italics added))

What I really like about this verse is the fact it uses simile and metaphor – *comparisons or figures of speech.* The adversary is like a lion, but he is *not* a lion. There is only one true Lion, and He is of the tribe of Judah.

⁴And I wept much, because no man was found worthy to open and to read the book, neither to look thereon. ⁵And one of the elders saith unto me, Weep not: behold, *the Lion of the tribe of Judah, the Root of David, hath prevailed to open the book, and to loose the seven seals thereof.* ⁶And I beheld, and, lo, *in the midst of the throne and of the four beasts, and in the midst of the elders, stood a Lamb as it had been slain,* having seven horns and seven eyes, which are the seven Spirits of God sent forth into all the earth.

(Revelation 5:4–6 (italics added))

We have to remain steadfast and stay focused on who has the victory. We do!

³And *every spirit that confesseth not that Jesus Christ is come in the flesh is not of God:* and this is that spirit of antichrist, whereof ye have heard that it should come; and even now already is it in the world. ⁴*Ye are of God, little children, and have overcome them: because greater is he that is in you, than he that is in the world.* ⁵They are of the world: therefore speak they of the world, and the world heareth them.

(1 John 4:3–5 (italics added))

Just remember how the devil was already defeated. He fell as lighting for all of his misdeeds. Ask God to preserve you, to wash you, and to keep you.

> [1]Have mercy upon me, O God, according to thy loving kindness: according unto the multitude of thy *tender mercies blot out my transgressions.* [2]*Wash me throughly from mine iniquity, and cleanse me from my sin.* [3]For I acknowledge my transgressions: and my sin is ever before me. [4]Against thee, thee only, have I sinned, and done this evil in thy sight: that thou mightest be justified when thou speakest, and be clear when thou judgest. [5]Behold, I was shapen in iniquity; and in sin did my mother conceive me. [6]Behold, *thou desirest truth in the inward parts:* and in the *hidden part thou shalt make me to know wisdom.* [7]*Purge me with hyssop, and I shall be clean: wash me, and I shall be whiter than snow.* [8]Make *me to hear joy and gladness; that the bones which thou hast broken may rejoice.* [9]Hide thy face from my sins, and blot out all mine iniquities. [10]*Create in me a clean heart, O God; and renew a right spirit within me.* [11]Cast me not away from thy presence; and take not thy holy spirit from me. [12]*Restore unto me the joy of thy salvation; and uphold me with thy free spirit.*
>
> (Psalm 5:1–12 (italics added))

CHAPTER 3

Lay Aside for the Fight

We know we are here to fight. As with all good fights, there is a contender and an opponent. The adversary is not our ally, *ever!* He is upset he was already defeated, and he still has not gotten over it. So it is his goal to bring as many with him as he possibly can. What we really need to know is hell is not intended for us, unless we just plan to go there. Oh yes, someone is going (i.e., the devil and his cohort), but make your election sure. Fight for your life, your eternal life.

¹Blessed be the LORD my strength which teacheth my hands to war, and my fingers to fight: ²My goodness, and my fortress; my high tower, and my deliverer; my shield, and he in whom I trust; who subdueth my people under me. *³LORD, what is man, that thou takest knowledge of him! or the son of man, that thou makest account of him.*

(Psalm 144:1–3 (italics added))

¹¹But thou, O man of God, flee these things; and *follow after righteousness, godliness, faith, love, patience, meekness.* *¹²Fight the good fight of faith, lay hold on eternal life,* whereunto thou art also called, and hast professed a good profession before many witnesses. *¹³I give thee charge in the sight of God, who quickeneth all things,* and before Christ Jesus, who before Pontius Pilate witnessed a good confession.

(I Timothy 6:11–13 (italics added))

I want you to think for a minute, if there is a good fight, is there also a bad fight? I have to say yes, because a bad fight is when we do anything which will hinder us from laying hold to eternal life. Think about it; you know better than I know if what you are doing will lead to the life God has preordained for you.

Here is where we separate fighting from warring. A fight is typically only for a short period of time. A war differs from a fight in that it is extensive and can proceed for days, months, or years. In the natural, when we prepare for war we first go through extensive Basic Training. The Scripture directs us how we are to go through Spiritual Basic Training. Essentially, we must get rid of any excess baggage which weighs us down and hinders God's plan.

I will refer to Spiritual Basic Training/boot camp as preparing ourselves physically, mentally, emotionally, and spiritually. It gives us the tools we need for the continuation of our journey for service. Not everyone will make it through this process, but its goal is to make us strong, or give us the right mindset—the mind of Christ.

Before even attempting this process, daily cardio *(heart exercises)* is necessary. Participants are required to get organized and focused for their training. We just talked about getting washed and cleansed in Psalm 51. After getting cleansed and ready, there are things we can not bring with us. We have to lay things aside as Hebrews 12:1–3 (italics added) stresses:

> [1]Wherefore seeing we also are compassed about with so great a cloud of witnesses, let us *lay aside every weight, and the sin which doth so easily beset us,* and let us *run with patience the race that is set before us,* [2]Looking unto Jesus *the author and finisher of our faith;* who for the joy that was set before him endured the cross, despising the shame, and is set down at the right hand of the throne of God. [3]For consider him that endured such contradiction of sinners against himself, lest ye be wearied and faint in your minds.

If an individual has questions when preparing for boot camp in the natural, they are to consult their recruiter. When we signed up for this *tour*, from the spiritual perspective, we were left with a manual—our Bible. We have to know for ourselves; read the Manual, so we will find answers to all questions with an assurance (He will never leave nor forsake us).

We have others who have made it before us; they are the great cloud of witnesses who are in heaven. They are forerunners who have successfully made it. They are at the end like a coach at a race, encouraging us to take another step, to press on toward the prize. Remember, if the great cloud of witnesses is not enough, there are people on the earth who are watching us, hoping we will make it. (Do not let trials and tribulations discourage you and cause you to slip.) *Press on!* Shake off the mess. In basic training, these obstacles are considered encumbrances (i.e., pets, friends, habits, and negative items which do not lead to our building up) hindrances.

> [19]These be they who separate themselves, sensual, having not the Spirit. [20]But ye, beloved, *building up yourselves on your most holy faith, praying in the Holy Ghost, [21]Keep yourselves in the love of God,* looking for the mercy of our Lord Jesus Christ *unto eternal life.*
> (Jude 1:19–21 (italics added))

If anything, we have to remember to get rid of weights *(impediments which way one down)*. Become cognizant of ensnarement or traps, which stem from people's actions. These things can take us from God's promises. (Hebrews 12:1–3 dictates we lay aside *every* weight.)

> [1]The elder unto the well beloved Gaius, whom I love in the truth. [2]Beloved, *I wish above all things that thou mayest prosper and be in health, even as thy soul prospereth.* [3]For I rejoiced greatly, when the brethren came and testified of the truth that is in thee, even as thou *walkest in the truth.*
> (III John 1:1–3 (italics added))

CHAPTER 4

Put on Jesus

Something I learned a while back is, it is considered inappropriate to wear multiple designers at the same time. To illustrate my point, if our shirt is one brand, our pants should also come from the same brand. If our athletic shoes are one brand, our socks should also match the brand. I say this to you because I want you to get the mindset we can not simultaneously put on multiple *garments.* If we are to consider this on a spiritual basis, we can not put on Christ and the world at the same time.

> *¹The Spirit of the Lord GOD is upon me;* because the LORD hath anointed me to preach good tidings unto the meek; he hath sent me to *bind up the brokenhearted,* to *proclaim liberty* to the captives, and the *opening of the prison* to them that are bound; ²To *proclaim the acceptable year of the LORD,* and the day of vengeance of our God; to *comfort all that mourn;* ³To appoint unto them that mourn in Zion, *to give unto them beauty for ashes,* the oil of joy for mourning, *the garment of praise* for the spirit of heaviness; *that they might be called trees of righteousness, the planting of the LORD, that he might be glorified.* ⁴And they shall build the old wastes, they shall raise up the former desolations, and they shall *repair the waste cities,* the desolations of many generations.
>
> (Isaiah 61(italics added))

Let me go further and say it in this manner, we can *not* serve two masters. We can try, but we are not going to do it well, and we will end up hating one. So which is it?

> [23]But if thine eye be evil, thy whole body shall be full of darkness. If therefore the light that is in thee be darkness, how great is that darkness! *[24]No man can serve two masters: for either he will hate the one, and love the other; or else he will hold to the one, and despise the other. Ye cannot serve God and mammon.* [25]Therefore I say unto you, *Take no thought for your life, what ye shall eat, or what ye shall drink;* nor yet for your body, what ye shall put on. Is not the life more than meat, and the body than raiment?
>
> (Matthew 6:23–25 (italics added))

> [13]Let us walk honestly, as in the day; not in rioting and drunkenness, not in chambering and wantonness, not in strife and envying. [14]But *put ye on the Lord Jesus Christ, and make not provision for the flesh,* to fulfill the lusts thereof.
>
> (Romans 13:13–14)

Do not seek opportunities to satisfy the flesh, no matter how small they appear. I will use an easy example for this. Some people are pros at *telling others off.* Remember Psalm 37:37–38, where we are told to *Mark the perfect man . . . .* I previously would ask God for a quicker whit . . . , I am fine. The Holy Ghost will not allow us to act certain ways (if we submit to Him). If we are a child of God, who is walking as we should, we will exemplify Christ. We must stop acting like we belong to someone else; either we are His or we are not. We are to let God direct us as to how we are to handle negative situations and people. We can not let the devil trick us out what God has for us.

> *[17]Recompense to no man evil for evil.* Provide things honest in the sight of all men. *[18]If it be possible,* as much as lieth in you, *live peaceably with all men.* [19]Dearly beloved, *avenge not yourselves, but rather give place unto wrath:* for it is written, *Vengeance is mine; I will*

repay, saith the Lord. [20]Therefore if thine enemy hunger, feed him; if he thirst, give him drink: for in so doing thou shalt heap coals of fire on his head. [21]*Be not overcome of evil, but overcome evil with good.*

(Romans 12: 17–21(italics added))

All we need to remember is if God is for us, He is more than enough. Let Him handle it.

[25]But thus saith the LORD, Even the captives of the mighty shall be taken away, *and the prey of the terrible shall be delivered: for I will contend with him that contendeth with thee, and I will save thy children.* [26]*And I will feed them that oppress thee with their own flesh;* and they shall be *drunken with their own blood,* as with sweet wine: and all flesh shall know that I the LORD am thy Saviour and thy Redeemer, the mighty One of Jacob.

(Isaiah 49:25–26 (italics added))

CHAPTER 5

Armor

I am thinking back to boot camp. After participating in basic training, we need to learn how to use our tools. Part of the concept of teaching our hands to war is learning how to use Scripture to fight the fight. Here is the armor God recommends for His children.

> [10]Finally, my brethren, *be strong in the Lord,* and in the power of his might. [11]*Put on the whole armour of God, that ye may be able to stand against the wiles of the devil. [12]For we wrestle not against flesh and blood, but against principalities, against powers, against the rulers of the darkness of this world, against spiritual wickedness in high places.* [13]Wherefore take unto you the *whole armour of God, that ye may be able to withstand in the evil day, and having done all, to stand.* [14]Stand therefore, having your *loins girt about with truth,* and having on the *breastplate of righteousness;* [15]And your *feet shod with the preparation of the gospel of peace;* [16]Above all, taking the *shield of faith,* wherewith ye shall be able to quench all the fiery darts of the wicked. [17]And take the *helmet of salvation,* and the *sword of the Spirit,* which is the word of God: [18]*Praying always with all prayer and supplication* in the Spirit, and watching thereunto with all perseverance and supplication for all saints;
>
> (Ephesians 6:10–18 (italics added))

Just because we are standing and the battling part belongs to the Lord, it does not mean we stand there and let the devil run over us. Armor in and of itself is a means for defense. Yes, God is handling things, but we are to take His Word and block, defend, or stand.

> [10]Finally, my brethren, be strong in the Lord, and in the power of his might. [11]Put on the whole armour of God, that ye may be able to stand against the wiles of the devil.
>
> (Ephesians 6:10–11(italics added))

I never did like getting in trouble as a child; you can believe I like it even less as an adult. To alleviate the possibility, I actively work on trusting and submitting my ways to *Him*. Remember, we are supposed to get our heart and mind in shape during boot camp.

> [5]Trust in the LORD *with all thine heart;* and lean *not unto thine own understanding.* [6]In all thy ways acknowledge him, and *he shall direct thy paths.* [7]Be not wise in thine own eyes: fear the LORD, and depart from evil.
>
> (Proverbs 3:5–7(italics added))

Put on is Greek—denotes urgency—demands immediate action. It does not imply to act like a doormat and concede. Our armor is for use. We can either use *all* of our armor or we can get beat up by our adversary, the devil.

> [12]For we wrestle not against flesh and blood, but against *principalities, against powers, against the rulers of the darkness of this world, against spiritual wickedness in high places.*
>
> (Ephesians 6:12 (italics added))

Wrestle lets us know we are fighting; it is used in hand-to-hand combat. It is used when we are on a lower level trying to take someone down, so they will *tap out*. The devil is the one we are fighting, not people. We may recognize a spirit, but remember it is not flesh and blood (the person). We are to use the authority God gave us. He said *whatsoever*; which encompasses everything.

[17]And if he shall neglect to hear them, tell it unto the church: but if he neglect to hear the church, let him be unto thee as an heathen man and a publican. [18]Verily I say unto you, *Whatsoever ye shall bind on earth shall be bound in heaven: and whatsoever ye shall loose on earth shall be loosed in heaven.* [19]Again I say unto you, That *if two of you shall agree* on earth as touching any thing that they shall ask, *it shall be done for them of my Father which is in heaven.*

(Matthew 18:17–19 (italics added))

Remember:

[4]Ye are of God, little children, and have overcome them: because *greater is he that is in you, than he that is in the world.*

(I John 4:4 (italics added))

[13]Wherefore take unto you the *whole armour of God,* that ye may be able to withstand in the evil day, and *having done all, to stand.* [14]Stand therefore, having your *loins girt about with truth, and having on the breastplate of righteousness;* [15]And *your feet shod with the preparation of the gospel of peace;* [16]Above all, taking the *shield of faith,* wherewith ye shall be able to *quench* (to dampen) *all the fiery darts of the wicked.*

(Ephesians 6:13–16 (italics added))

We have to have the faith of God to believe we are more than a conqueror, and we will win.

[17]Even so *faith, if it hath not works, is dead, being alone.* [18]Yea, a man may say, Thou hast faith, and I have works: shew me thy faith without thy works, and I will *shew thee my faith by my works.* [19]Thou believest that there is one God; thou doest well: the

33

devils also believe, and tremble. [20]But wilt thou know, O vain man, that *faith without works is dead?*

(James 2:17–20 (italics added))

One must believe God's Word. Through faith use your shield. If you saw the movie *300*, think about the purpose of the army's shield. The shied blocks those arrows the adversary is trying to shoot at us in order to wound or kill us. Yes, I said kill. The devil is playing for keeps. Put God's Word on him, do not play his games. While we are in this war, make sure you wear your helmet. A helmet is to protect our head, so we can keep our focus on God, so we can protect our minds. We must keep our thoughts right. A helmet is for protection, but a sword is for fighting. Use the Word of God to put the devil in his place . . . stomped under our feet.

[17]And *take the helmet of salvation, and the sword of the Spirit, which is the word of God.*

(Ephesians 6:17 (italics added))

This might feel like a touchy subject, but I want to remind you of something. Salvation is needed if one wants to fight against the adversary. The devil will not fight against himself.

[22]And the scribes which came down from Jerusalem said, He hath Beelzebub, and by the prince of the devils casteth he out devils. [23] And he called them unto him, and said unto them in parables, *How can Satan cast out Satan?* [24] And if *a kingdom be divided against itself,* that kingdom *cannot stand,*

(Mark 3:22–24 (italics added))

If we want to become successful in battle, we have to use God's Word to fight. Using the appropriate scripture for a particular situation is how we adequately apply Rhema (certain verses for certain times) not Logos.

[18]Praying *always with all prayer and supplication in the Spirit,* and watching thereunto *with all perseverance and supplication for all saints.*

(Ephesians 6:18)

Praying is grammatically linked to *stand* – we can not stand if we are not praying. The bottom line is we are not as effective if we are not praying and applying the Word of God as needed. We must remain vigilant. Do not get tired; we have to keep fighting even when we do not feel like we can take it; fight! Because:

[1]Blessed be the LORD *my strength which teacheth my hands to war, and my fingers to fight.*

(Psalm 144:1 (italics added))

CHAPTER 6

Killing the Flesh

Our flesh is one of our biggest opponents. We must not become consumed with its operation.

> [5]For *they that are after the flesh do mind the things of the flesh;* but *they that are after the Spirit the things of the Spirit.* [6]For to be *carnally minded is death;* but to be *spiritually minded is life and peace.*
>
> (Romans 8:5–14 (italics added))

I know there are times when we may feel we must *straighten* out a situation, but I say we can not think or respond like the world. We are not controlled by a *worldly mind* but by a *spiritual mind-set*. If you are not trying to make preparation to rule and reign with the Heavenly Father upon the return of Jesus, keep doing what you are doing. I am making plans for the future. We are mandated to get our minds off the world; we are to place them on God.

> [7]Because *the carnal mind is enmity against God:* for it is not subject to the law of God, neither indeed can be.
>
> (Romans 8:7 (italics added))

It is this simple; we are either spiritually minded or carnally minded. Just for clarity, enmity is defined as enemy.

[8]So then they that *are in the flesh cannot please God.*

(Romans 8:8 (italics added))

As stated in a previous chapter, when we walk in the flesh, we also put ourselves back into condemnation. We are implored to not walk after our flesh.

[1]There is therefore *now no condemnation to them which are in Christ Jesus,* who walk not after the flesh, but after the Spirit.

(Romans 8:1 (italics added))

[9]But *ye are not in the flesh, but in the Spirit,* if so be that the Spirit of God dwell in you. Now *if any man have not the Spirit of Christ, he is none of his.*

(Romans 8:9 (italics added))

He is our friend, so why would we want to jeopardize our walk, our friendship, our relationship with God by getting in and operating in the flesh. We just read (Romans 8:9), we are not His if we walk contrary to the verse. Question: . . . if you do not have His Spirit, how can He recognize you to help you? It comes down to have you offered up a prayer of repentance? If so, you have moved into the relationship mode. It is like a parent that comes to the aid of their child. It is one thing to see someone else's child in trouble, but when it is your child . . . you get the picture. Again, it comes down to ownership and relationship with God. I have had individuals dispute what we just read, but I will make it plain with the next text reference.

[31]Now we know that God *heareth not sinners: but if any man be a worshipper of God, and doeth his will, him he heareth.*

(John 9:31 (italics added))

You ask, do you need the Holy Spirit? If you want a relationship, yes! Here is some simple math for you:

You + the Spirit of Christ = ownership/relationship

> [10]And if Christ be in you, *the body is dead because of sin; but the Spirit is life because of righteousness.* [11]But if the Spirit of him that raised up Jesus from the *dead dwell in you,* he that raised up Christ from the *dead shall also quicken your mortal bodies by his Spirit that dwelleth in you.* [12] Therefore, brethren, *we are debtors, not to the flesh, to live after the flesh.* [13]*For if ye live after the flesh, ye shall die: but if ye through the Spirit do mortify the deeds of the body, ye shall live.* [14]For as many as are *led by the Spirit of God, they are the sons of God.* [15]For ye have not received the spirit of bondage again to fear; but ye have received the *Spirit of adoption,* whereby we cry, *Abba, Father.*
>
> (Romans 8:10–15 (italics added))

I like it when I find out an individual has been adopted. The reason being is with adoption an individual is selected. It is one thing to just have a child, but it is a totally different ball game when we go through the process and select one. What do you think? I like having received *the Spirit of adoption, whereby we cry, Abba.* Once we become a part of the family, we become enlightened as to how the family business is run.

Because we are standing upright, He is not going to let us struggle through by ourselves. I used this scripture reference before, but it bares repeating,

> [10] For a day in thy courts is better than a thousand. I had rather be a doorkeeper in the house of my God, than to dwell in the tents of wickedness. [11]For the LORD God is a sun and shield: the LORD will give grace and glory: *no good thing will he withhold from them that walk uprightly.* [12] O LORD of hosts, blessed is the man that trusteth in thee.
>
> (Psalm 84:10–12 (italics added))

If we are walking upright, we are not ruled by our flesh or sin. This walk is about eternal life. He also said we are debtors. A debtor owes. If we do not owe the flesh, who do we owe? Exactly, *we owe God!* We can either separate ourselves from sin, or we can let sin separate us from God. (I choose to work on my relationship with God and not let sin separate me.) Back to the adopting a child analogy, we can and will do only so much for someone else's child, but when they belong to us, we go all the way for them.

> [37]Mark the perfect (blameless) man, and *behold the upright: for the end of that man is peace.* [38]But the transgressors shall be destroyed together: the end of the wicked shall be cut off. [39]But *the salvation of the righteous is of the LORD: he is their strength in the time of trouble.* [40]And *the LORD shall help them,* and *deliver them:* he shall deliver them from the wicked, and *save them,* because *they trust in him.*
> (Psalms 37:37–40 (emphasis and italics added))

> [10]*I the LORD search the heart* (innermost being), *I try* (test) *the reins,* (mind – literally the most secret parts) even *to give every man according to his ways, and according to the fruit of his doings* – deeds.
> (Jeremiah 17:10 (emphasis and italics added))

> [19]Dearly beloved, *avenge not yourselves, but rather give place unto wrath:* for it is written, *Vengeance is mine; I will repay, saith the Lord.* [20]Therefore *if thine enemy hunger, feed him; if he thirst, give him drink: for in so doing thou shalt heap coals of fire on his head.* [21]*Be not overcome of evil, but overcome evil with good.*
> (Romans 12:19–21 (italics added))

These are powerful scriptures. Go back to these scriptures and meditate on them; hide them in your heart. I want you to get your reward, and not get in trouble. Let God direct your path. He knows the way we take. Just fight the good fight, hide God's Word in your heart, and remember to whom we belong.

People are watching our walk; we may not see them, but they definitely see us. My father often talks about how we are so easily identified. We do not have to tell people we our God's child;

we have a neon sign on our forehead indicating it. Our walk may cause someone to reevaluate their actions, because we have become a living testimony. I have given you a lot to contemplate by sharing these scriptures.

> [13]*Take fast hold of instruction; let her not go:* keep her; for she is thy life. [14]*Enter not into the path of the wicked, and go not in the way of evil men.* [15]Avoid it, pass not by it, turn from it, and pass away. [16]For *they sleep not, except they have done mischief;* and *their sleep is taken away, unless they cause some to fall.* [17]For they eat the bread of wickedness, and drink the wine of violence. [18]But *the path of the just is as the shining light, that shineth more and more unto the perfect day.* [19]The way of the wicked is as darkness: they know not at what they stumble. [20]*My son, attend to my words; incline thine ear unto my sayings.* [21]*Let them not depart from thine eyes; keep them in the midst of thine heart.* [22]*For they are life unto those that find them, and health to all their flesh.*
>
> (Proverbs 4:13–22 (italics added))

Stand therefore . . . having . . . . If you do not yet see reason for having the Holy Spirit operating in your life, pray and seek God for direction. He will not lead you wrong, and after seeking Him, wait on Him.

> [8]Finally, be ye all of one mind, having compassion one of another, love as brethren, be pitiful, be courteous: [9]Not rendering evil for evil, or railing for railing: but contrariwise blessing; knowing that ye are thereunto called, that ye should inherit a blessing. [10]For he that will love life, and see good days, let him refrain his tongue from evil, and his lips that they speak no guile: [11]Let him eschew evil, and do good; let him seek peace, and ensue it. [12]*For the eyes of the Lord are over the righteous, and his ears are open unto their prayers: but the face of the Lord is against them that do evil.* [13]And who is he that will harm you, if ye be followers of that which is good? [14]But and if ye suffer for righteousness' sake, happy are ye: and be not afraid of their

terror, neither be troubled; *15But sanctify the Lord God in your hearts: and be ready always to give an answer to every man that asketh you a reason of the hope that is in you with meekness and fear:* 16Having a good conscience; that, whereas they speak evil of you, as of evildoers, they may be ashamed that falsely accuse your good conversation in Christ. 17For it is better, if the will of God be so, that ye suffer for well doing, than for evil doing. 18For Christ also hath once suffered for sins, the just for the unjust, that he might bring us to God, being put to death in the flesh, but quickened by the Spirit: 19By which also he went and preached unto the spirits in prison; 20Which sometime were disobedient, when once the longsuffering of God waited in the days of Noah, while the ark was a preparing, wherein few, that is, *eight souls were saved by water.* 21The like figure whereunto even *baptism doth also now save us* (not the putting away of the filth of the flesh, but the answer of a good conscience toward God,) *by the resurrection of Jesus Christ:* 22Who is gone into heaven, and is on the right hand of God; angels and authorities and powers being made subject unto him.

(I Peter 3:8–22 (italics added))

27But the anointing which *ye have received of him abideth in you,* and ye need not that any man teach you: but as *the same anointing teacheth you of all things, and is truth,* and is no lie, and even as it hath taught you, ye shall abide in him.

(I John 2:27 (italics added))

If the Holy Spirit is abiding in us, as we say He is, *we already have the answers we need dwelling inside us.* If what is being spewed out the mouths of others does not line up with God's Word or what the Holy Spirit is leading us to do, than we can not receive the instruction; there are those who are false. If they are not for us, then they are against us. Remember, *greater is He* and other scriptures which pertain to your situation.

>⁶Who also hath made us able ministers of *the* new testament;
not of *the letter,* but of *the spirit:* for *the letter killeth,* but *the* spirit
giveth life.
>
>(II Corinthians 3:6 (italics added))

We have to remember we have rivers of living water coming
out our vessel. We have all kinds of potential waiting on us to
activate and use it. We must stir up the gift which resides deep
down inside us.

>³⁸*He that believeth on me,* as the scripture hath said, *out of his belly*
shall flow *rivers of living water.*
>
>(John 7:38 (italics added))

Also,

>⁵When I call to remembrance the *unfeigned faith* that is in thee,
which dwelt first in thy grandmother Lois, and thy mother
Eunice; and I am persuaded that in thee also. ⁶Wherefore I put
thee in remembrance that thou *stir up the gift of God, which is in
thee* by the putting on of my hands. ⁷For *God hath not given us the
spirit of fear; but of power, and of love, and of a sound mind.*
>
>(II Timothy 1:5–7 (italics added))

We have got to use what we already have. One of the best scriptures
I can link to this thought process is Luke 12:47–49 (italics added):

>⁴⁷And that servant, which *knew his lord's will,* and prepared
not himself, *neither did according to* his will, *shall be beaten with
many stripes.* ⁴⁸But he that knew not, and did commit things
worthy of stripes, shall be beaten with few stripes. *For unto
whomsoever much is given, of him shall be much required:* and to
whom men have committed much, of him they will ask the
more. *⁴⁹I am come to send fire on the earth;* and what will I, if it
be already kindled?

So if we know much is required of us, than we must apply it. We can take our choice from any of the 66 Books. Speak the Scripture and see how the Word comes alive in your life, in your situation. Step back and watch God (not you) change the situation. We can not move to the next assignment or level until we first handle the current state of affairs. We need to surround ourselves with the Word, whether it is coming through reading the Bible, listening to songs, or listening to sermons. He said to hide the Word inside, and expect Him to hold up His end. He will not disappoint us no matter what comes our way; God is greater than our circumstances.

> [10]With my whole heart have I sought thee: O let me not wander from thy commandments. [11]Thy word *have I hid in mine heart, that I might not sin against thee.* [12]Blessed art thou, O LORD: teach me thy statutes.
>
> (Psalm 119: 10–12 (italics added))

He forewarned perilous times will come.

> [1]This know also, that *in the last days perilous times shall come.* [2]For men shall be *lovers of their own selves, covetous, boasters, proud, blasphemers, disobedient to parents, unthankful, unholy, [3]Without natural affection, trucebreakers, false accusers, incontinent, fierce, despisers of those that are good,*
>
> (II Timothy 3: 1–3 (italics added))

But in spite of, if you need more reassurance, just ask David. He said it well.

> [23]*The steps of a good man are ordered by the LORD: and he delighteth in his way.* [24]Though he fall, he shall not be utterly cast down: for the LORD upholdeth him with his hand. [25]*I have been young, and now am old; yet have I not seen the righteous forsaken, nor his seed begging bread.*
>
> (Psalm 37:23–25 (italics added))

For backup support, look at the following:

> [5]Let *your* conversation be without covetousness; and be content with such things as ye have: for he hath said, *I will never leave thee, nor forsake thee.*
>
> (Hebrew 13:5 (italics added))

We have to meditate on God's Word, His promises. Look at what He said He will do for us.

> [1]Blessed is the man that *walketh not in the counsel of the ungodly, nor standeth in the way of sinners,* nor sitteth in the seat of the scornful. [2]But his delight is in the law of the LORD; and in *his law doth he meditate day and night.* [3]And he shall be like a tree planted by the rivers of water, that bringeth forth his fruit in his season; his leaf also shall not wither; and whatsoever he doeth shall prosper.
>
> (Psalm 1:1–3 (italics added))

Put Him back in remembrance of what He said.

> [25]I, even I, am he that blotteth out thy transgressions for mine own sake, and *will not remember thy sins.* [26]*Put me in remembrance: let us plead together: declare thou, that thou mayest be justified.*
>
> (Isaiah 43:25–26 (italics added))

He will do for us, if we please Him. The more we hear the Words of our God, the more it will resonate within us. We will come to rely on it. We will start to flex our faith muscles, and they will continue to grow the more we depend on God's Word.

> [17]So then *faith cometh by hearing, and hearing by the word of God.*
>
> (Romans 10:17 (italics added))

This repeated hearing of the Word will help us to put things in the proper perspective. (Strive to associate with individuals who can help to build up your faith.)

> *¹⁹These be they who separate themselves, sensual, having not the Spirit.* ²⁰But ye, beloved, *building up yourselves on your most holy faith,* praying in the Holy Ghost, ²¹Keep yourselves in the love of God, looking for the mercy of our Lord Jesus Christ unto eternal life.
>
> (Jude 1:19–21 (italics added))

Okay, so now we are listening and meditating on the Word of God through various venues. *Building up* implies we are taking the Word and working it for our benefit. Think of a weight lifter and how they meticulously prepare for a competition. They build themselves by watching what they put in and on their bodies. They guard every morsel they consume. In like manner, we are to cautiously take things into our ear-gates, weighing each item to see and determine whether it is fit for consumption. I want to encourage you to become a doer of the Word of God.

> ¹²For as many as have sinned without law shall also perish without law: and as many as have sinned in the law shall be judged by the law; *¹³For not the hearers of the law are just before God, but the doers of the law shall be justified.* ¹⁴For when the Gentiles, which have not the law, do by nature the things contained in the law, these, having not the law, are a law unto themselves.
>
> (Romans 2:12–14 (italics added))

Doing encompasses more than taking in the Word; doing is the epitome of the walk. We have to prepare for this battle. The adversary is not taking a vacation, *ever!* We have been told to walk by faith.

> ⁶Therefore we are *always confident,* knowing that, whilst we are at home in the body, we are absent from the Lord: *⁷(For we walk by faith, not by sight:)* ⁸We are confident, I say, and willing rather to be absent from the body, and to be present with the Lord.
>
> (II Corinthians 5:6–8 (italics added)

So we are becoming engulfed with faith through our actions. I remind you, we may have our focus on God, but the adversary will pinpoint his focus on us. Remember earlier where we discussed I Peter 5:6–8. He is prowling and seeking whom he may devour. Just like roaches, we know his imps will come out the woodwork. They will try to pull on us and convince us to go contrary to the Word, but we must become persuaded by God's Word.

> ³⁶As it is written, For thy sake we are killed all the day long; we are accounted as sheep for the slaughter. ³⁷Nay, in all these things *we are more than conquerors through him that loved us.* ³⁸For I am *persuaded, that neither death, nor life, nor angels, nor principalities, nor powers, nor things present, nor things to come,* ³⁹Nor height, nor depth, nor any other creature, shall be able to separate us from the love of God, which is in Christ Jesus our Lord.
>
> (Romans 8:36–39 (italics added))

> ¹²For the which cause I also suffer these things: nevertheless I am not ashamed: *for I know whom I have believed,* and *am persuaded that he is able to keep that which I have committed* unto him against that day. ¹³*Hold fast the form of sound words,* which thou hast heard of me, in faith and love which is in Christ Jesus.
>
> (II Timothy 1:12–13 (italics added))

Hold on, tie a not in it, do not become dissuaded, but become persuaded. No one is saying it is easy. The adversary never played fair; he wants to get us off track and to doubt what God has told us. God warns us not to fall for the enemy's tricks—moving from one side of the fence to the other. Stand solid on His Word. The more we become afflicted, the more we have to hunker down, know without a doubt we win. We are in this fight for the long haul. In the end, God will show us His pleasure in our service.

> [14]That we henceforth be no more children, tossed to and fro, and *carried about with every wind of doctrine, by the sleight of men, and cunning craftiness,* whereby they lie in wait to deceive; [15]But speaking the truth in love, may grow up into him in all things, which is the head, even Christ:
>
> (Ephesians 4:14–15 (italics added))

> [26]Then shall ye begin to say, We have eaten and drunk in thy presence, and thou hast taught in our streets. [27]But he shall say, I tell you, *I know you not whence ye are; depart from me, all ye workers of iniquity.* [28]*There shall be weeping and gnashing of teeth,* when ye shall see Abraham, and Isaac, and Jacob, and all the prophets, in the kingdom of God, and you yourselves thrust out.
>
> (Luke 13:26–28 (italics added))

The fight is on; we do not have to take the devil's blows. We are to *fight the good fight,* not stand back like wimps and just take it.

We are also told *violence is coming, but we have to ready ourselves to take back what is ours.* We know we are to stand. Standing does not mean taking it, it means defending it (God's Word; what He thinks and says about us) and being ready at all times to move at His directive. You may ask, *"What if He doesn't tell me to move?"* Well, I guess you will just need to continue to hold your critical position until He does direct. I have a question for you; are you missing His direction? Only you know the true answer. If you have asked a question, is it the right question? His Word states we do not have answers for a reason.

> [23]And in that day ye shall ask me nothing. Verily, *verily, I say unto you, Whatsoever ye shall ask the Father in my name, he will give it you.* [24]Hitherto have ye asked nothing in my name: ask, and ye shall receive, that your joy may be full. [25]These things have

I spoken unto you in proverbs: but the time cometh, when I shall no more speak unto you in proverbs, but I shall shew you plainly of the Father.

(John 16:23–25 (italics added))

²Ye lust, and have not: ye kill, and desire to have, and cannot obtain: ye fight and war, yet ye have not, because ye ask not. ³Ye ask, and receive not, because ye ask amiss, *that ye may consume it upon your lusts. ⁴Ye adulterers and adulteresses, know ye not that the friendship of the world is enmity with God? Whosoever therefore will be a friend of the world is the enemy of God.*

(James 4:2–4 (italics added))

Wait on the Lord and *be of good courage.*

¹³I had fainted, unless I had believed to see the goodness of the LORD in the land of the living. ¹⁴Wait on the LORD: be of good courage, and *he shall strengthen thine heart: wait, I say, on the LORD.*

(Psalm 27:13–14 (italics added))

Waiting does not imply sitting around doing nothing. Waiting is about staying prayerful and connected so when He does instruct, we are ready and prepared to do thus saith the Lord. I also want to highlight the word good. If we can *be of good courage* than the opposite *be of bad courage* must also exist. Which are you choosing?

Let me switch gears at this point. I want to swing toward why what is happening is happening. I want to strongly state sometimes things happen, and it is not because we did something to cause it to happen. If we are walking uprightly, there are times when warfare will occur. It is not our fault, but it can become our solution.

¹⁸The LORD is *nigh unto them that are of a broken heart;* and saveth such as be of a contrite spirit. *¹⁹Many are the afflictions of the*

righteous: but the LORD delivereth him out of them all. [20]He keepeth all his bones: not one of them is broken.

(Psalm 34:18–20 (italics added))

The righteous will have times of suffering. It may appear others have it easier, but He is working things for our good.

[16]For which cause we faint not; but though our outward man perish, yet the inward man is renewed day by day. [17]*For our light affliction, which is but for a moment, worketh for us a far more exceeding and eternal weight of glory;* [18]While we *look not at the things which are seen,* but at the things which are not seen: for the *things which are seen are temporal;* but the things which are not seen are eternal.

(II Corinthians 4:16–18 (italics added))

Things may cease to exist and seasons may change, but despite what we do and do not understand, we are to trust God.

[4]So shalt thou *find favour and good understanding in the sight of God and man.* [5]*Trust in the LORD with all thine heart; and lean not unto thine own understanding.* [6]In all thy ways acknowledge him, and he *shall direct thy paths.*

(Proverbs 3:4–6 (italics added))

As I mentioned earlier in my writing, we are more than a conqueror. Wait on the Lord, and trust in Him. While you are at it, ask Him to teach you His ways and what you are to learn so you do not have to repeat the negative.

[2]*O my God, I trust in thee: let me not be ashamed, let not mine enemies triumph over me.* [3]*Yea,* let none that wait on thee be ashamed: *let them be ashamed which transgress without cause.* [4]*Shew me thy ways, O LORD; teach me thy paths.*

(Psalm 25:2–4 (italics added))

When people are working against us without cause, we are to let God handle it. Bring Him in remembrance of Psalm 25. Whatever we do, we must realize we are not in control; stop worrying. This is God's battle. Learn from how God handled situations in the past for His people. (Not only did He tell them what, but He told them when, where, and how.)

> ¹⁴Then upon Jahaziel the son of Zechariah, the son of Benaiah, the son of Jeiel, the son of Mattaniah, a Levite of the sons of Asaph, came the Spirit of the LORD in the midst of the congregation; ¹⁵And he said, Hearken ye, all Judah, and ye inhabitants of Jerusalem, and thou king Jehoshaphat, *Thus saith the LORD unto you, Be not afraid nor dismayed by reason of this great multitude; for the battle is not yours, but God's.* ¹⁶To morrow go ye down against them: behold, they come up by the cliff of Ziz; and ye shall find them at the end of the brook, before the wilderness of Jeruel.
>
> (II Chronicles 20:14–16 (italics added))

Yes, it may appear great, but God can handle it better than we ever could dream to handle it.

CHAPTER 7

Storms

Often times when we go through a storm, the storm may seem as if it is never-ending. We may have finished the actual process, the storm finally ends, but we still find ourselves suffering from the by-product or residue of the storm. We may even find ourselves in a state of dislocation. Let us look at Isaiah 25 for how the Word deals with our storms.

> *¹O Lord, thou art my God; I will exalt thee,* I will *praise thy name;* for thou hast done wonderful things; thy counsels of old are *faithfulness* and *truth.* *²For thou hast made of a city an heap; of a defenced city a ruin: a palace of strangers to be no city; it shall never be built.* *³Therefore shall the strong people glorify thee, the city of the terrible nations shall fear thee.* ⁴For thou hast been a *strength to the poor, a strength to the needy in his distress, a refuge from the storm,* a shadow from the heat, when the blast of the terrible ones is as a storm against the wall. *⁵Thou shalt bring down the noise of strangers, as the heat in a dry place; even the heat with the shadow of a cloud:* the branch of the *terrible ones shall be brought low.*
>
> (Isaiah 25:1–5 (italics added))

God will deal with the storms which we face. He has even said how the oppressors will get brought low. What person wants to suffer at the hand of the Almighty God? Not me, and I hope you too are saying, *"Not I."* God does promise to deliver us from the storm, but I want to remind you our time is not like His time. It is not always an overnight process. Just like the passing of a hurricane, the restoration after the storm takes time. Sometimes, we may feel as if we are still in the heat of a battle, the eye of a storm, but perhaps it is just the residue.

When the enemy tries to come in like a flood, what did God promise to do?

> [18]According to their deeds, *accordingly he will repay, fury to his adversaries, recompence to his enemies; to the islands he will repay recompence.* [19]So shall they fear the name of the LORD from the west, and his glory from the rising of the sun. *When the enemy shall come in like a flood, the Spirit of the LORD shall lift up a standard against him.* [20]And the Redeemer shall come to Zion, and unto them that turn from transgression in Jacob, saith the LORD.
>
> (Isaiah 59:18–20 (italics added))

When we are going through a storm, we must speak to the situation and keep the faith. As Jesus did, we will have to tell it *Peace be still*. Do not wait until after it is over; speak to the storm during the highs as well as during the lows. Several years ago there was a song which started, *"I've been in the storm too long."* No matter what, we must keep our focus and see ourselves making it out the situation victorious. My greatest example of these two thoughts is Mark 4:38–40 (italics added):

> [38]And he was in the hinder part of the ship, asleep on a pillow: and they awake him, and say unto him, *Master, carest thou not that we perish? [39]And he arose, and rebuked the wind, and said unto the sea, Peace, be still.* And the wind ceased, and there was a great calm. [40]And *he said unto them, Why are ye so fearful? how is it that ye have no faith?*

Does the Lord care we are still going through? *Carest thou not . . . .* Yes, He said He will *never leave us nor forsake us.* While we are in it,

He is with us. We are to keep our focal point—our eyes—upon Jesus. Do not get side tracked. God cares. Speak to your situation; tell Him what you need; pray the scripture. Do you know we are the apple of His eye? We are to stay anchored down all throughout the trying situations, the storms of life. Thomas Whitfield sings, *My soul has been anchored in the Lord.* Are you anchored? When the winds are blowing and the seas are tossed to and fro, are you doing like the disciples did? Are you worrying, or are you having faith in God?

It does not matter how strong the storm, it is not our fight. As stated earlier,

> [15]And he said, Hearken ye, all Judah, and ye inhabitants of Jerusalem, and thou king Jehoshaphat, Thus saith the LORD unto you, *Be not afraid nor dismayed by reason of this great multitude; for the battle is not yours, but God's.*
>
> (II Chronicles 20:15 (italics added))

God is always faithful to His children; He will come through for us.

> [22] It is of *the LORD'S mercies that we are not consumed,* because his *compassions fail not.* [23] They are *new every morning: great is thy faithfulness.* [24] *The LORD is my portion,* saith my soul; therefore will I hope in him.
>
> (Lamentations 3:22–24 (italics added))

No one is saying the adversary is fair; he is going to come against us and try us. We just need to remember the purpose of the roar. I Peter 5:7–9 (italics added) first reminds us we have a caring God, and we are to give Him every situation:

> [7]*Casting all your care upon him; for he careth for you. [8]Be sober, be vigilant; because your adversary the devil, as a roaring lion, walketh*

about, seeking whom he may devour: ⁹Whom *resist stedfast* in the faith, knowing that the same afflictions are accomplished in your brethren that are in the world.

As a is not indicative of *is*. The purpose of the roar is to get us to come from under our covering, to jump or respond in fear to the situation. Once we come from under what we know God says about us, the adversary tries to pounce. The thing is, God pulled his teeth a long time ago when He took the keys. We have to remember the devil is a sore loser. He has no teeth, and he can only swing at us. It is up to us if we are going to use the *shield of faith* to quench all those fiery blows he throws and swings our way. Utilize the sword, which is the Word of God. Do not give him place in your storm.

A companion scripture is for us *not to give place* to the adversary. Sometimes a situation or storm can cause all kinds of feeling to arise in us. After we have given God the storm/situation/care, we need to watch what tries to take our focus off God.

> ²⁶*Be ye angry, and sin not: let not the sun go down upon your wrath:* ²⁷*Neither give place to the devil.* ²⁸Let him that stole steal no more: but rather let him labour, working with his hands the thing which is good, that he may have to give to him that needeth.
>
> (Ephesians 4:26–28 (italics added))

Getting upset and harboring ill feelings can lead to anger and wrath. Again, this battle is not ours. I will remind you of what David did to Goliath. Let us go to 1 Samuel 17:46–51(italics added):

> ⁴⁶*This day* will the LORD deliver thee into mine hand; and I will smite thee, and take thine head from thee; and I will give the carcases of the host of the Philistines this day unto the fowls of the air, and to the wild beasts of the earth; *that all the earth*

may know that there is a God in Israel. [47]And *all this assembly shall know that the LORD saveth not with sword and spear: for the battle is the LORD's,* and he will give you into our hands. [48]And it came to pass, when the Philistine arose, and came, and drew nigh to meet David, that David hastened, and ran toward the army to meet the Philistine.

[49]And David *put his hand in his bag, and took thence a stone, and slang it, and smote the Philistine in his forehead, that the stone sunk into his forehead; and he fell upon his face to the earth.* [50]So *David prevailed* over the Philistine with a sling and with a stone, and smote the Philistine, and slew him; but there was no sword in the hand of David. [51]Therefore David ran, and stood upon the Philistine, and took his sword, and drew it out of the sheath thereof, and slew him, and cut off his head therewith. And when the Philistines saw their champion was dead, they fled.

David used what God gave him. He believed what God said about him, made a decree, and stood strong to prevail over the enemy. David could have gotten distracted in the situation and lost his focus. After it was over, he finished off the enemy and left. What we did not see David do was stay there and get into a recall situation of how wrong he was treated by the enemy.

When we go through conflicts—storms—*we are to go through* and not wallow in them. I am not saying it is easy to leave it all behind. But we have to see ourselves as God sees us, and not stay in the battle, even after it is over. Move forward!

[13]Brethren, *I count not myself to have apprehended:* but this one thing I do, *forgetting those things which are behind,* and *reaching forth* unto those *things which are before,* [14]*I press toward the mark for the prize of the high calling of God in Christ Jesus.* [15] Let us therefore, as many as be perfect, *be thus minded:* and if in any thing ye be otherwise minded, God shall reveal even this unto you.

(Philippians 3:13–15 (italics added))

What I am saying is there is no need to habitually reflect on past storms and belittle individuals afterward. Some of our enemies are just waiting to see how we respond, so they can attempt to tear down our witness. Carefully proceed; they may have been God's child and have fallen from good standing with the Savior. I could apply a lot of scriptures here, but I will choose only one.

> [1]Brethren, *if a man be overtaken in a fault, ye which are spiritual, restore such an one in the spirit of meekness; considering thyself, lest thou also be tempted.* [2]Bear ye one another's burdens, and so fulfill the law of Christ. [3]For *if a man think himself to be something, when he is nothing, he deceiveth himself.*
>
> (Galatians 6:1–3 (italics added))

Another thing to watch for is do not become surprised if we have speculators and spectators watching to see how we handle ourselves after a storm. Let them watch and learn. This is not to say we should repeatedly address a situation. Shake off the dust and move. After all, we will have other storms and battles. We do not owe anyone an answer, and it is not profitable to tear down the other party(s) involved. The object is to go through and not have to repeatedly go through because we did not learn the entire process the first time. Remember God's Word.

> [19]Dearly beloved, *avenge not yourselves, but rather give place unto wrath:* for it is written, *Vengeance is mine; I will repay, saith the Lord.*
>
> (Romans 12:19 (italics added))

He is going to take care of it. They may think they have gotten by, but they will not get away. He is going to repay, which means we do not go around running our mouths tearing down someone else's name. We know better. How do I know? I am telling you now, we will reap it according to the next seven verses, which follow the text I just used.

¹Brethren, if a man be *overtaken in a fault, ye which are spiritual, restore such an one in the spirit of meekness; considering thyself, lest thou also be tempted.* ²Bear ye one another's burdens, and so fulfil the law of Christ. ³For *if a man think himself to be something, when he is nothing, he deceiveth himself.* ⁴But let every man prove his own work, and then shall he have rejoicing in himself alone, and not in another. ⁵For *every man shall bear his own burden.* ⁶Let him that is taught in the word communicate unto him that teacheth in all good things. ⁷*Be not deceived; God is not mocked: for whatsoever a man soweth, that shall he also reap.* ⁸*For he that soweth to his flesh shall of the flesh reap corruption; but he that soweth to the Spirit shall of the Spirit reap life everlasting.* ⁹And let us not be weary in well doing: *for in due season we shall reap, if we faint not.* ¹⁰As we have therefore opportunity, *let us do good unto all men, especially unto them who are of the household of faith.*

(Galatians 6:1–10 (italics added))

Due season—is it your time? If you do not have it yet, it is not your time.

We have to stop posting all our business and the business of others for everyone to see and hear. Sometimes, we might get a little urge to want to *help* God. Do not get in trouble! Helping is almost a guarantee we are going to go through our rough spot even longer. Do not pay because you *just had to help.* We have to stop interfering in things which are not any of our concern. By so doing, we are acting against ourselves, and I assure you it gets ugly quick, fast, and in a hurry. Just remember the hymnal which encourages us to *be not dismayed whatever betithes* . . . . God will take care of His people. If you are not His, then do what you have to do. I am thinking, if you are reading this text, you are His.

When people do us wrong and we continue to harbor ill feelings for them, we let them win (and they win again each time we rehash it and let it consume us). They appear to have won when they did it; remember to whom the vengeance belongs. When we continue to *suffer* because of what they did, we are giving place to the adversary. Ask God to teach you how to release whatever occurred. He does not want it showing on our face, in our walk, and in our talk day in and day out for the rest of our lives. We are more than a conqueror, because He said so in Romans the eighth chapter.

> ³⁶As it is written, For thy sake we are *killed all the day long; we are accounted as sheep for the slaughter.* ³⁷*Nay, in all these things we are more than conquerors through him that loved us.* ³⁸For I am *persuaded,* that neither death, nor life, nor angels, nor principalities, nor powers, nor things present, nor things to come, ³⁹*Nor height, nor depth, nor any other creature, shall be able to separate us from the love of God, which is in Christ Jesus our Lord.*
>
> (Romans 8:36–39 (italics added))

We have got to get persuaded because we are not just a conqueror but more than a conqueror, and nothing is going to disconnect us from His love. *Nothing,* and *no one.* Yes it hurt, but God is our provider, and He will take care of us. He said, *"all these things"* meaning it is not just a little thing which is trying to affect us and stop us from living a life victorious. He has great love for you, child of the Living God. Whose report are we going to believe? Okay, whose report should we believe? I say I am going to believe the report of the Lord.

> ¹⁵And how shall they preach, except they be sent? as it is written, How beautiful are the feet of them that preach the gospel of peace, and bring glad tidings of good things! ¹⁶But they have not all obeyed the gospel. For Esaias saith, Lord, *who hath believed our report?* ¹⁷*So then faith cometh by hearing, and hearing by the word of God.*
>
> (Romans 10:15–17 (italics added))

One of the areas in which Christians have challenges is in the area of forgiveness. Forgiveness is a part of *all these things.* We just said we will let nothing separate us. Does the nothing include the evil act someone committed against us? His Word states we are to *forgive others their debts.* There is no stipulation on the debt. A debt is something people owe us. Even if they never ask our forgiveness, guess what we are supposed to do? Forgive! If I am not mistaken, He said something like a whole bunch of times.

> [21]Then came Peter to him, and said, Lord, how *oft shall my brother sin against me, and I forgive him?* till *seven times?* [22]Jesus saith unto him, I say *not unto thee, Until seven times: but, Until seventy times seven.*
>
> (Matthew 18:21–22 (italics added))

The reasoning behind forgiveness has absolutely nothing to do with the next person. The bottom line is, we are trying to remain in the right place with God. How can we expect our Father to just let us slide with every little thing we do against Him, and we can not forgive our brothers or sisters? Do inventory. The big kicker on this Scripture reference is so He will forgive us our debts. If we do not forgive, we do not allow Him to forgive. Check out what the Bible states. Go with me to Matthew.

> [6]But thou, *when thou prayest, enter into thy closet,* and when thou hast *shut thy door, pray to thy Father* which is in secret; and *thy Father which seeth in secret shall reward thee openly.* [7]But when ye pray, use *not vain repetitions, as the heathen do:* for they *think that they shall be heard for their much speaking.* [8]Be not ye therefore like unto them: for *your Father knoweth what things ye have need of, before ye ask him.* [9]After this manner therefore pray ye: Our Father which art in heaven, Hallowed be thy name. [10]*Thy kingdom come, Thy will be done in earth, as it is in heaven.* [11]*Give us this day our daily bread.* [12]And *forgive us our debts, as we forgive our debtors.* [13]And lead us not into temptation, but deliver us from evil: For thine is the kingdom,

and the power, and the glory, for ever. Amen. [14]For if ye forgive men their trespasses, your heavenly Father will also forgive you: [15]But if ye forgive not men their trespasses, neither will your Father forgive your trespasses. [16]Moreover when ye fast, be not, as the hypocrites, of a sad countenance: for they disfigure their faces, that they may appear unto men to fast. Verily I say unto you, *They have their reward.* [17]*But thou, when thou fastest, anoint thine head, and wash thy face;* [18]*That thou appear not unto men to fast,* but unto thy Father which is in secret: and thy Father, which seeth in secret, shall reward thee openly.

(Matthew 6:6–18 (italics added))

You may think, "How many scriptures is she going to use?" As I said initially, I want you to take God's Word, not my word, and hide it in your heart. Many times I have heard people say we do not have to forget. I have even heard of people saying specifically to forgive and not to forget. I will even say there was a time when I absolutely agreed with them. But lo and behold *life* taught me differently. Recently, I have heard multiple preachers saying we must forgive. So I started doing research on it, which is when I had to refer back to Matthew six. Give us this day our daily bread. We all like this reference, but we need to skip to the next verse *and forgive that our debts . . . ,* which is a leading statement. How can He forgive us? We have done some unthinkable things to other people who are also God's children.

We know when someone says something to our children or does something wrong to them, all we want to do is go get them. Yet, when we do things to children of our Lord and Savior, we do not want Him to have the same policy. Correct? We want Him to go back to the Old Testament where He states He will wash us as white as snow. That is extra special! Do we know why He tells us to forgive others? It is so when we mess up we can go to Him boldly as His child. We are to put Him in remembrance of Scripture, which tells Him to forgive us as we forgive others.

Correct; forgive us. He says, when something is washed, we can not see what was previously on it. So in a sense we want our Lord to forget we *messed up*. Hmm . . . we want Him to do something we are not willing to do for our brother and sister in Christ? This sounds like a double standard—hypocritical. You choose whichever one is easier to digest.

So, now we are willing to forgive and forget, are we not? I must say at this point, when we forgive it does not mean for us to start hanging out with the person who did the offense. It means simply to restore them to their previous stance before the offense was committed. Do you remember how earlier I stated how we are to come to the point where we repeatedly forgive even for multiple offenses? He knows when we do not forgive, we encumber/impede ourselves. The bottom line is about our keeping it so God will continue to forgive us. It is about us, not them. God is so amazing! He works out our misdeeds prior to their occurrences. He knows we are going to do things, but He makes allocations for us. If we want Him to forgive and forget, we better do likewise. I know. I can hear you saying, "But you don't know what they did to me!" Yeah. But I do know as long as you keep focusing on *what they did* to you, you are in danger of moving to the next level past unforgiveness . . . offense. The Scripture is also clear on this area. Get off our knees at the altar and *go to our brother or sister and get the situation straightened out and* then *go back to God.*

> [23]Therefore if thou bring thy gift to the altar, *and there rememberest that thy brother hath ought against thee;* [24]*Leave there thy gift before the altar,* and go thy way; *first* be reconciled to thy brother, and *then* come and offer thy gift. [25]*Agree with thine adversary quickly,* whiles thou art in the way with him; lest at any time the adversary deliver thee to the judge, and the judge deliver thee to the officer, and thou be cast into prison.
>
> (Matthew 5:23–25 (italics added))

The truth of the matter is, we have business we need to handle . . . first things first.

> ^{31}Now we know that God *heareth not sinners:* but *if any man be a worshipper of God, and doeth his will, him he heareth.*
>
> (John 9:31(italics added))

> ^{32}*I came not to call the righteous, but sinners to repentance.*
>
> (Luke 5:32 (italics added))

> ^{9}He that *turneth away his ear from hearing the law,* even *his prayer shall be abomination.*
>
> (Proverbs 28:9 (italics added))

> ^{47}*He that is of God heareth God's words:* ye therefore hear them not, because ye are not of God.
>
> (John 8:47)

He is not hearing prayers of sinners anyway, when we are in offense. And while we are at it, if we think our brother needs help, *Ye who are spiritual* are to restore them in love. Get your business straight. Guess what? We are not to publish all the details of the situation we are rectifying either. It is nobody's business. Do we want to get a prayer through? It is funny how many people want to say, "I'm praying for you." But going back to the Bible, my question is *with unforgiving hearts,* sinning, and remaining in offense, are the *prayers heard?* Again, we must get ourselves aligned with God's Word. It is not whether God wants to answer our prayers; it is a matter of *honoring His Word above his name.*

Forgive does not mean a matter did not take place; it is simply *not repeatedly focusing on something.* Forgiveness is seeing the person through the Blood of Jesus (washing), not through the fault. Do not let someone convince you not to forgive, they are totally against

Scripture. It really is not anyone else's concern how and how many times we forgive . . . *seventy times seven*. Again, when we do not forgive an act, it simply weighs us down and hinders God from responding/moving on our behalf.

CHAPTER 8

Did Flesh and Blood Reveal It?

Now I am about to turn to a subject some individuals do not want to accept. Watch for people speaking into your life. Weigh anything said. By so doing, we will know if a person is telling the truth and if they are the true prophet of God. They do not have to ask us what we think of what they spoke unto us. Sometimes people take the little pieces of information we give them and use it. All I am suggesting is just watch for individuals trying to misuse their gifts.

There are so many people with gifts I have actually become leery of individuals wanting to speak a prophetic word into my life. Gifting does not require a question and answer session in order for someone to tell us what God has told them. Do we recall this happening in Biblical times? Or do we just remember God sending a direct Word to a specific person or group? People with gifts have to watch so they do not get nosy. Certain ones want to know more than they need to know. It is like they are misusing their gift(s). I know God's Word states *the gifts and calling of God* come without repentance.

> ²⁷For this is my covenant unto them, when I shall take away their sins. ²⁸As concerning the gospel, they are enemies for your

sakes: but as touching the election, they are beloved for the father's sakes. *29For the gifts and calling of God are without repentance.* 30For as ye in times past have not believed God, yet have now obtained mercy through their unbelief.

(Romans 11:27–30 (italics added))

A true prophet will not need us to assist them. If it comes to pass, then we know they were a true prophet. We live in treacherous times, and people will try to manipulate the Word. I have used the book of Matthew a lot, but it is especially fitting here.

12Therefore all things whatsoever ye would that men should do to you, do ye even so to them: for this is the law and the prophets. *13Enter ye in at the strait gate: for wide is the gate, and broad is the way, that leadeth to destruction, and many there be which go in thereat:* 14Because strait is the gate, and narrow is the way, which leadeth unto life, and few there be that find it. *15Beware of false prophets, which come to you in sheep's clothing,* but inwardly they are ravening wolves. *16Ye shall know them by their fruits.* Do men gather grapes of thorns, or figs of thistles? 17Even so every good tree bringeth forth good fruit; but a corrupt tree bringeth forth evil fruit. *18A good tree cannot bring forth evil fruit,* neither can a corrupt tree bring forth good fruit. 19Every tree that bringeth not forth good fruit is hewn down, and cast into the fire. 20Wherefore by their fruits ye shall know them. *21Not every one that saith unto me, Lord, Lord, shall enter into the kingdom of heaven;* but he that doeth the will of my Father which is in heaven. *22Many will say to me in that day, Lord, Lord, have we not prophesied in thy name? and in thy name have cast out devils? and in thy name done many wonderful works?* 23And then will I profess unto them, *I never knew you: depart from me, ye that work iniquity.*

(Matthew 7:12–23 (italics added))

Occurrences are going to arise in all of our lives, but just remember to have faith in God and not in man. According to Psalm 91, He will hide us in those times of trouble. I would like to recommend whatever you are going through, do not let it consume you. Trouble comes to pass, not to stay. We are to make wise choices for our lives; weigh the consequences of our choices or lack of action. Sometimes, not doing anything will cost us more than we are willing to pay. So we are to choose in wisdom. Ask God for wisdom, and He will *give it liberally.*

> ⁴But let patience have her perfect work, *that ye may be perfect and entire, wanting nothing.* ⁵*If any of you lack wisdom, let him ask of God, that giveth to all men liberally, and upbraideth not;* and it shall be given him. ⁶But let him *ask in faith, nothing wavering. For he that wavereth is like a wave of the sea driven with the wind and tossed.*
>
> (James 1:4–6 (italics added))

When we look back on the current times we are facing, are we going to look back with regret? Are we going to realize how we depended on God's Word? Is He going to say we followed what He said?

> ²²It is of the LORD's mercies that we are not consumed, because his compassions fail not. ²³They are new every morning: *great is thy faithfulness.*
>
> (Lamentations 3:22–23 (italics added))

Another outcome of going through a storm is our increased development. We may even look back on our situation and say we do not get it. Rest assured, it is not always for us to get, but God does reveal what He wants us to know. Sometimes it is even just bringing clarity to why or how. It may even come after the fact, but He sometimes even gives us an understanding of occurrences and motives behind them. No matter your situation, I want to remind you to remain prayerful. We are to pray God's Word back to Him, so we can put Him in *remembrance* of promises made to the children of God.

⁵Let your conversation be without covetousness; and be content with such things as ye have: for he hath said, *I will never leave thee, nor forsake thee. ⁶So that we may boldly say, The Lord is my helper, and I will not fear what man shall do unto me.*

(Hebrews 13:4–6 (italics added))

There are many promises found throughout the Bible, but I will leave this one with you.

¹The LORD is my shepherd; I shall *not want.* ²He maketh me to *lie down in green pastures: he leadeth me* beside the still waters. ³He *restoreth* my soul: he leadeth me in the paths of righteousness for his name's sake. ⁴Yea, though I walk through the valley of the shadow of death, I will *fear no evil:* for thou art *with me;* thy rod and thy staff they *comfort me.* ⁵Thou *preparest a table before me in the presence of mine enemies:* thou *anointest my head with oil;* my cup runneth over. ⁶Surely *goodness and mercy shall follow me all the days of my life:* and I will *dwell in the house of the LORD* for ever.

(Psalm 23:1–6 (italics added))

Whose report are we going to believe . . . man's or God's?

At the same time, I want to encourage you to also take your problems to God and leave them there. I will attest, this takes practice. Leaving our problems is connected to the scripture, *Cast your cares . . . .* It is all about careful aim. Additionally, do not put someone else in the place of our Savior. No helpers are required. Need I remind you, He is a jealous God?

¹⁴Ye shall not go after other gods, of the gods of the people which are round about you; ¹⁵(For the LORD *thy God is a jealous God* among you) *lest the anger of the LORD thy God be kindled against thee,* and destroy thee from off the face of the earth. ¹⁶Ye shall not tempt the LORD your God, as ye tempted him in Massah.

(Deuteronomy 6:14–16 (italics added))

When one keeps running to others and not run to God, carefully proceed. When problems arise, it is no time to stop praising God. On the contrary, we need to praise Him more. He said *He will keep us in perfect peace.*

> ²Open ye the gates, that the righteous nation which keepeth the truth may enter in. *³Thou wilt keep him in perfect peace, whose mind is stayed on thee: because he trusteth in thee. ⁴Trust ye in the LORD for ever: for in the LORD JEHOVAH is everlasting strength:*
> (Isaiah 26:2–4 (italics added))

Another scripture to support this mindset projects we are to bless Him no matter what.

> *¹I will bless the LORD at all times: his praise shall continually be in my mouth.* ²My soul shall make her boast in the LORD: the humble shall hear thereof, and be glad. ³O magnify the LORD with me, and let us exalt his name together.
> (Psalm 34:1–3 (italics added))

There is not a stipulation on when and why, it just is. It is not just for when times are going well. We want to keep our focus on God so He can keep our minds together and at peace. Is this not one of His promises? We can even say keep us sane. It is about keeping our mind, soul, and body healthy while we are going through the hard press, the hard trial. Keeping our mind stayed/focused on Him also enables us to hear Him when He is ready to move us. Stand, stand, and stand some more. Hold your position, ready to proceed at His directive.

I will share with you when I was going through one of the biggest battles of my life, God eventually removed me from the situation for a temporary time of rest. With the removal, I was able to refocus back on God. The trial was great, but He was able to organize or orchestrate circumstances for my good. Praise God!

There is nothing like God removing His child from a battle, so He can protect them. I am thinking about Psalm 91 again here. He will hide us under His shadow to cool things and ease the pressure. There is *no one* who can do it better than God.

> [1]He that *dwelleth in the secret place* of the *most High* shall *abide under the shadow of the Almighty.* [2]I will say of the LORD, *He is my refuge and my fortress: my God; in him will I trust.* [3]Surely he *shall deliver thee from the snare of the fowler,* and from the noisome pestilence. [4]*He shall cover thee with his feathers, and under his wings shalt thou trust: his truth shall be thy shield and buckler.* [5]Thou *shalt not be afraid for the terror by night;* nor for the arrow that flieth by day; [6]*Nor for the pestilence that walketh in darkness;* nor for the destruction that wasteth at noonday. [7]*A thousand shall fall at thy side, and ten thousand at thy right hand; but it shall not come nigh thee.* [8]Only with thine eyes shalt thou behold and see the reward of the wicked. [9]*Because thou hast made the LORD,* which is my refuge, even the most High, *thy habitation;* [10]There shall *no evil befall thee,* neither shall any plague come nigh thy dwelling. [11]For *he shall give his angels charge over thee, to keep thee in all thy ways.* [12]They shall *bear thee up in their hands,* lest thou dash thy foot against a stone. [13]Thou shalt tread upon the lion and adder: the young lion and the dragon shalt thou trample under feet. [14]Because *he hath set his love upon me,* therefore will I deliver him: *I will set him on high, because he hath known my name.* [15]He shall call upon me, and I will answer him: I will be with him in trouble; I will deliver him, and honour him. [16]*With long life will I satisfy him, and shew him my salvation.*
>
> (Psalm 91: 1–16 (italics added))

The Bible talks about how a false prophet came along and told the prophet of God to go a certain way God told him not to go. As a result, the prophet followed the word and direction of the false prophet. Of course, it cost him. You can just guess what happened. I King 13:7–24 (italics added) will provide further insight:

⁷And the king said unto the man of God, Come home with me, and refresh thyself, and I will give thee a <u>reward</u>. *⁸And the man of God said unto the king, If thou wilt give me half thine house, I will not go in with thee, neither will I eat bread nor drink water in this place: ⁹For so was it charged me by the word of the Lord, saying, Eat no bread, nor drink water, nor turn again by the same way that thou camest.* ¹⁰So he went another way, and returned not by the way that he came to Bethel. ¹¹Now there dwelt an *old prophet in Bethel;* and his sons came and told him all the works that the man of God had done that day in Bethel: the words which he had spoken unto the king, them they told also to their father. ¹²And their father said unto them, What way went he? For his sons had seen what way the man of God went, which came from Judah. ¹³And he said unto his sons, Saddle me the ass. So they saddled him the ass: and he rode thereon, *¹⁴And went after the man of God, and found him sitting under an oak: and he said unto him, Art thou the man of God that camest from Judah? And he said, I am. ¹⁵Then he said unto him, Come home with me, and eat bread.* ¹⁶And he said, I *may not return with thee, nor go in with thee:* neither will I eat bread nor drink water with thee in this place: ¹⁷For it was said to me by the word of the Lord, Thou shalt eat no bread nor drink water there, nor turn again to go by the way that thou camest. *¹⁸He said unto him, I am a prophet also as thou art; and an angel spake unto me by the word of the Lord, saying, Bring him back with thee into thine house, that he may eat bread and drink water. But he lied unto him. ¹⁹So he went back with him, and did eat bread in his house, and drank water.* ²⁰And it came to pass, as they sat at the table, that the word of the Lord came unto the prophet that brought him back: *²¹And he cried unto the man of God that came from Judah, saying, Thus saith the Lord, Forasmuch as thou hast disobeyed the mouth of the Lord, and hast not kept the commandment which the Lord thy God commanded thee, ²²But camest back, and hast eaten bread and drunk water in the place, of the which the Lord did say to thee, Eat no bread, and drink no water; thy carcase shall not come unto the sepulchre of thy fathers.* ²³And it came to pass, after he had eaten bread, and after he had drunk, that he saddled for him the ass, to wit, for the prophet whom he had brought back.

²⁴ *And when he was gone, a lion met him by the way, and slew him: and his carcase was cast in the way, and the ass stood by it, the lion also stood by the carcase.*

Of course, death followed as a result of going according to the wrong leading of the supposed *man of God.* When God is using people, remember sometimes it is only for a season. The Holy Spirit is provided for a comfort. When we are going through life, the *Comforter is come . . .* to comfort, but He also speaks, clarifies, and reveals. We may want to go as we think we ought to, but we need to make sure it is by the leading of God, through the Holy Spirit.

Do you know God can and will provide individuals to assist us on our journey, and it is up to us how much we do and do not share with them? If they are led of the Holy Spirit, they will have enough leading to deliver the message from God. They will not have to delve into our business in order for us to receive support, especially when they are prophetic. If they are so prophetic, we will not have to tell them anything . . . they do not need us to tell, co-sign, validate. Again, if they are a true prophet it will come to pass. I have even had prophetic individuals complain about my level of transparency. The devil is liar and the father of lies. I do not have to tell you my business. Just do what thus saith the Lord. It truly is no one's business, unless we *just have to* share. The problem with telling all our business is when we forgive people; others will not forget the things we shared with them.

Share what you have been released to share, and watch God move. *Obedience is* always *better than sacrifice.* This scripture pertains to another situation in life, but it is still applicable here.

²¹But the people took of the spoil, sheep and oxen, the chief of the things which should have been utterly destroyed, to sacrifice unto the LORD thy God in Gilgal. ²²And Samuel

said, Hath the LORD as great delight in burnt offerings and sacrifices, as in obeying the voice of the LORD? *Behold, to obey is better than sacrifice, and to hearken than the fat of rams. ²³For rebellion is as the sin of witchcraft, and stubbornness is as iniquity and idolatry.* Because thou hast rejected the word of the LORD, he hath also rejected thee from being king.

(1 Samuel 15:21–23 (italics added))

If we do it God's way, others will sit back in wonder and know beyond a shadow of doubt it was *only* God who was able to work out the situation. We may wonder, but they will sit in wonder when it is orchestrated by God. After all, it is simple; He wants us to *be in health and prosper*—not in stress—*even as our souls prosper.* Amen, and it is so.

¹The elder unto the well beloved Gaius, whom I love in the truth. *²Beloved, I wish above all things that thou mayest prosper and be in health, even as thy soul prospereth.* ³For I rejoiced greatly, when the brethren came and testified of the truth that is in thee, even as thou walkest in the truth.

(III John 1:1–3 (italics added))

I keep going back to the importance of casting all our cares on Him and taking a solid stand. God will sustain us while we are going through our storms. I know we may not necessarily want things to transpire the way they have, but just *trust* God.

Do you remember Hurricane Katrina? Do you know anyone from Louisiana? Well, I want to associate devastating storms of life with Katrina. Those who experienced it will tell us another account of what happened and will never forget the hurricane. How many people do we know who went through Katrina and were so devastated they were forced to change their previous lifestyle and relocate? The storm has long sense passed, but they are still suffering from the residue of the storm. Look back at Scripture. Paul came in on *broken pieces of the shipwreck.*

> [41]And falling into a place where two seas met, they ran the ship aground; and the forepart stuck fast, and remained unmoveable, but the hinder part was broken with the violence of the waves. [42]And the soldiers' counsel was to kill the prisoners, lest any of them should swim out, and escape. [43]But the centurion, willing to save Paul, kept them from their purpose; and commanded that they which could swim should cast themselves first into the sea, and get to land: [44]*And the rest, some on boards, and some on broken pieces of the ship.* And so it came to pass, that *they escaped all safe to land.*
>
> (Acts 27: 41–44 (italics added))

He made it through, but he was greatly impacted by the storm. He had even previously been *bit by vipers.*

> [2]And the barbarous people shewed us no little kindness: for they kindled a fire, and received us every one, because of the present rain, and because of the cold. [3]And when Paul had gathered a bundle of sticks, and laid them on the fire, *there came a viper out of the heat, and fastened on his hand.* [4]And when the barbarians saw the venomous beast hang on his hand, they said among themselves, No doubt this man is a murderer, whom, though he hath escaped the sea, yet vengeance suffereth not to live.
>
> (Acts 28:2–4 (italics added))

While in the midst of our storms, we can not take our focus off God. Just like Peter when he stepped onto the water, have faith God is with us and will not fail us. Even when the storm totally subsides, we can not let the residue of the storm overwhelm us. The aftermath is sometimes just as great and powerful as the storm itself. Stay prayed up and focused on God. Know from where our *help comes.*

> *[1]I will lift up mine eyes unto the hills, from whence cometh my help. [2]My help cometh from the LORD, which made heaven and earth.* [3]He will not suffer thy foot to be moved: he that keepeth thee will not slumber.

(Psalm 121:1–3 (italics added))

CHAPTER 9

Guard Your Heart

God is amazing in how He allows His people to receive insight and hints, if they are in tune and listening. Granted, this is not every time, but if we have *an ear to hear* what He is saying it can save us a lot of heartache. Yes, we would like to have audible signs of what is to come to pass, but when we do not know what to do we are to refer to the Word. What does it say about your situation? We do not have to have a Word and a confirming Word on what God is directing us to do. Take Him at His Word. Know *the battle is not ours,* but God's, as He said in II Chronicles 20:14–16.

If the battle does not belong to us, we will need to spend extra time seeking His face, connecting to him, leaning on *His everlasting arm.* I can go to David's writings when he shared *never seen the righteous forsaken, nor His seed begging bread* in Psalm 37:24 – 26. Also, we are *more than a conqueror* through our Lord and Savior in Romans 8:36–38.

Watch so you do not just let anyone speak into your life. I just mentioned how cunning the enemy is, how he will use anyone. This includes from the supposed people of God to the people on the streets. *Guard your heart.*

> [23]Keep thy heart with all diligence; for out of it are the *issues of life.* [24]Put away from thee a froward mouth, and perverse lips

put far from thee. ²⁵Let thine eyes look right on, and let thine eyelids look straight before thee. *²⁶Ponder the path of thy feet, and let all thy ways be established. ²⁷Turn not to the right hand nor to the left: remove thy foot from evil.*

(Proverbs 4:23–27 (italics added))

When I was in my storm, the fourth chapter of Proverbs kept coming to me. Again, if it does not align with God's *plan,* or will not *prosper us* as indicated throughout Scripture, then we can not let it in our ears. More importantly, we can not let it in our heart. Whatever we do, we can not take it into our heart because *out of it flows the issues of life.* Why do you think the enemy wants to twist our hearing and blur our vision? Keep both tuned into Jesus. Know prospering us does not always equate to resolving the situation to our satisfaction. God knows the *plans He has for us,* and it will *work for our good* (even when it may appear we are losing the fight). He told us to *fight the good fight of faith,* but know the battle is still not ours.

¹⁰For thus saith the LORD, That after seventy years be accomplished at Babylon I will visit you, and *perform my good word toward you,* in causing you to return to this place. *¹¹For I know the thoughts that I think toward you, saith the LORD, thoughts of peace, and not of evil, to give you an expected end. ¹²Then shall ye call upon me, and ye shall go and pray unto me, and I will hearken unto you. ¹³And ye shall seek me, and find me, when ye shall search for me with all your heart.*

(Jeremiah 29:10–13 (italics added))

²⁷And *he that searcheth the hearts knoweth what is the mind of the Spirit, because he maketh intercession for the saints according to the will of God.* ²⁸And we know that all things work together for good to them that love God, to them who are the called according to his purpose. ²⁹For whom he did foreknow, he also did predestinate to be conformed to the image of his Son, that he might be the firstborn among many brethren.

(Romans 8:27–29 (italics added))

While we are in battle, we must stay not only spiritually fit, but also take care of our physical temple. God's Word states *exercise profits* us little, but I want the little it does profit me.

> [7]But refuse profane and old wives' fables, and exercise thyself rather unto godliness. *[8]For bodily exercise profiteth little: but godliness is profitable unto all things,* having promise of the life that now is, and of that which is to come. [9]This is a faithful saying and worthy of all acceptation.
>
> (I Timothy 4:7–9 (italics added))

Also, we are to *present our bodies a living sacrifice;* this includes eating healthy and getting proper sleep. It also includes being fervent in business. Multiple times, I have been told Kingdom business requires haste. Whether it is your business or God's business, take care of it in a timely manner.

> [1]I beseech you therefore, brethren, by the mercies of God, that ye *present your bodies a living sacrifice, holy, acceptable unto God, which is your reasonable service.* [2]And be not conformed to this world: but be ye transformed by the renewing of your mind, *that ye may prove what is that good, and acceptable, and perfect, will of God.* [3]For I say, through the grace given unto me, to every man that is among you, not to think of himself more highly than he ought to think; but to think soberly, according as God hath dealt to every man the measure of faith.
>
> (Romans 12:1–3 (italics added))

So properly handle your business. We do not want or need unnecessary stress to ride into the storm, also. So get organized, and take care of your matters. One of my favorite scriptures concerning business is to *consider the ways of the ant old sluggard.*

> [5]Deliver thyself as a roe from the hand of the hunter, and as a bird from the hand of the fowler. *[6]Go to the ant, thou sluggard; consider her ways, and be wise:* [7]Which having no guide, overseer,

or ruler, *⁸Provideth her meat in the summer, and gathereth her food in the harvest. ⁹How long wilt thou sleep, O sluggard?* When wilt thou arise out of thy sleep? ¹⁰Yet a little sleep, a little slumber, a little folding of the hands to sleep.

(Proverbs 6:5–10 (italics added))

If our timing is off and we do not do what we are directed to do, we should not become surprised if opportunities pass by us. Some opportunities only come once, and if we let them pass us by we can not blame it on God. Question . . . is it due to not totally trusting and believing *God will do what He said He will do?* We have heard the phrase timing is everything; it definitely applies to the way we regulate our lives.

So as items are revealed, do not resist what is revealed personally through the Spirit. Know God is a gentleman, and He is not going to always come to us holding up a billboard sign. He is not going to always blare at us what we are to or not to do. *He that hath an ear* comes into play again here.

⁸And other fell on good ground, and did yield fruit that *sprang up and increased; and brought forth, some thirty, and some sixty, and some an hundred.* ⁹And he said unto them, *He that hath ears to hear, let him hear.* ¹⁰And when he was alone, they that were about him with the twelve asked of him the parable.

(Mark 4:8–10 (italics added))

Do not resist what He is revealing; it will just prolong the storm. Denial is not the best option when we are in a storm. One thing is certain, when we seek *counsel in a multitude* and think we can trust them, we do not know what we are going to get. Seek God. It is not best for us to run to everyone telling them every detail of our lives.

³⁷After this man rose up Judas of Galilee in the days of the taxing, and drew away much people after him: he also perished; and all,

> even as many as obeyed him, were dispersed. [38]And now I say
> unto you, *Refrain from these men, and let them alone:* for if this counsel
> or this work be of men, it *will come to nought:* [39]*But if it be of God, ye
> cannot overthrow it;* lest haply ye be found even to fight against God.
> (Acts 5:37–39 (italics added))

Again, I go back to how can we expect everyone else to forgive if
we have unnecessarily shared information? People have a tendency
to remember the minute details when we do not want them to
remember. Especially when we have moved on to the next level
in God; do not let your confession or sharing sessions turn into
hindrances and roadblocks for others. Make your decisions, and
deal with the *enemy quickly,* know what spirit is using the person. It
is the adversary, not them, using them. Refer to Matthew 5:24–26.

Do not allow others to become your *little Jesus* and tell you every
move to make. If it is, *"thus saith the Lord"* it does not matter what
others think we think. I advise you to know God is no respecter of
person. We are to ask ourselves, is there a motive behind other's
words or actions? Whether they are the person creating the trials/
storms, or if they are the person delivering prophesy to . . . , is
there an ulterior motive? They will have to give an account.

> [35]A good man out of the good treasure of the heart bringeth
> forth good things: and *an evil man out of the evil treasure bringeth
> forth evil things.* [36]But I say unto you, That every idle word that
> men shall speak, they shall give account thereof in the day of
> judgment. [37]For by thy words thou shalt be justified, and by thy
> words thou shalt be condemned.
> (Matthew 12:35–37 (italics added))

God can speak to and through anyone; just look at *Balaam and the
donkey* he was riding. God can speak if we are willing to hear. When
hurtful things are said, do not quickly disregard the message. I
remember one time I was in the middle of a lesson, and a student

spoke something to me (someone who was not the best example of character) in front of a class full of students. I was floored and denied the possibility of what was spoken. In retrospect, they were correct, and I wish I had regarded what was said and addressed it. Hindsight, . . . learn from my mistake.

> ^{21}And Balaam rose up in the morning, and saddled his ass, and went with the princes of Moab. ^{22}And God's anger was kindled because he went: and the angel of the LORD stood in the way for an adversary against him. Now he was riding upon his ass, and his two servants were with him. ^{23}And the ass saw the angel of the LORD standing in the way, and his sword drawn in his hand: and the ass turned aside out of the way, and went into the field: and Balaam smote the ass, to turn her into the way. ^{24}*But the angel of the LORD stood in a path of the vineyards, a wall being on this side, and a wall on that side. ^{25}And when the ass saw the angel of the LORD, she thrust herself unto the wall, and crushed Balaam's foot against the wall: and he smote her again.* ^{26}And the angel of the LORD went further, and stood in a narrow place, where was no way to turn either to the right hand or to the left. ^{27}And *when the ass saw the angel of the LORD, she fell down under Balaam: and Balaam's anger was kindled, and he smote the ass with a staff. ^{28}And the LORD* opened the mouth of the ass, and she said unto Balaam, What have I done unto thee, that thou hast smitten me these three times? ^{29}And Balaam said unto the ass, Because thou hast mocked me: I would there were a sword in mine hand, for now would I kill thee. ^{30}And the ass said unto Balaam, Am not I thine ass, upon which thou hast ridden ever since I was thine unto this day? was I ever wont to do so unto thee? and he said, Nay. ^{31}*Then the LORD* opened the eyes of Balaam, and he saw the angel of the *LORD* standing in the way, and his sword drawn in his hand: and he bowed down his head, and fell flat on his face.
> (Numbers 22:21–31 (italics added))

On the other hand, items are also delivered by individuals who simply *profess* they are children of God, and they are simply trying to hurt us with their words. Know people by their fruit, and take it (whatever it is) to *God in prayer.* I have heard people say so many times how God does *not want us to judge people so we ourselves are not judged.* Well, it is true; we are not to *sit in the seat of judgment,* but He did ordain for us to perform as active fruit inspectors—see Matthew 7:13–20.

As fruit/motives are revealed, ask God if He wants you to commune or *break bread with people.* It does not matter if they are ministers of His gospel; He may tell us not to break bread. Again, *obedience is* so much *better than sacrifice.* If we do not know, we are to ask God. If we lack wisdom in anything, ask Him and He will *give us wisdom.* God is protective of His sheep. Yes, we are His sheep; He will even come after us if needed. Remember, it is our obligation to *know His voice,* not a stranger's.

> [4]And when he putteth forth his own sheep, *he goeth before them, and the sheep follow him: for they know his voice.* [5]*And a stranger will they not follow,* but *will flee from him:* for they know not the voice of strangers. [6]This parable spake Jesus unto them: but they understood not what things they were which he spake unto them.
>
> (John 10:4–6 (italics added))

> [26]But ye believe not, because ye are not of my sheep, as I said unto you. [27]*My sheep hear my voice, and I know them, and they follow me:* [28]And I give unto them eternal life; and they shall never perish, neither shall any man pluck them out of my hand.
>
> (John 10:26–28 (italics added))

If anything, remember *God is a jealous God,* and He does not take kindly to our seeking others when we are to seek Him. *Seek ye first the kingdom of God, and His righteousness.*

> [30]Wherefore, if God so clothe the grass of the field, which to day is, and to morrow is cast into the oven, shall he not

much more clothe you, O ye of little faith? [31]Therefore take no thought, saying, What shall we eat? or, What shall we drink? or, Wherewithal shall we be clothed? [32](For after all these things do the Gentiles seek:) for your heavenly Father knoweth that ye have need of all these things. [33]*But seek ye first the kingdom of God, and his righteousness; and all these things shall be added unto you.* [34]Take therefore no thought for the morrow: for the morrow shall take thought for the things of itself. Sufficient unto the day is the evil thereof.

(Matthew 6:30–34 (italics added))

What is the Kingdom? *Righteousness, peace, joy in the Holy Ghost.*

[16]Let not then your good be evil spoken of: [17]*For the kingdom of God is not meat and drink; but righteousness, and peace, and joy in the Holy Ghost.* [18]For he that in these things serveth Christ is acceptable to God, and approved of men.

(Romans 14:16–18 (italics added))

Ask Him for His direction. If we need clarity on His directives, we are to pray and ask for revelation. He wants to *commune with us*; we are *the apple of His eye.* He wants us to cast it, as I stated earlier in the text. *Cast our cares on Him.* Bring our troubles to God and leave them there. We have got to love God more than we love anything or anyone else. I can not stress this point strongly enough. We can not even have *the appearance of evil* in this area.

[21]*Prove all things; hold fast that which is good.* [22]*Abstain from all appearance of evil.* [23]And the very God of peace sanctify you wholly; and I pray God your whole spirit and soul and body be preserved blameless unto the coming of our Lord Jesus Christ.

(I Thessalonians 5:21–23 (italics added))

I am the last one to deny life will serve hurtful situations to us. If you have not experienced any form of hurt, just keep on living and I assure you . . . . As long as there are professors of the Word (people who profess to, but do not exemplify God's Word) there are opportunities to become hurt. No matter what, *walk in love.* God actually wants us to *walk in the spirit* so we do not *fulfill the lust of the flesh.*

> [2]Wherein in time past ye walked according to the course of this world, according to the prince of the power of the air, the spirit that now worketh in the children of disobedience: [3]Among whom also we all had our conversation in times past in the lusts of our flesh, fulfilling the desires of the flesh and of the mind; and were by nature the children of wrath, even as others. [4]But *God, who is rich in mercy, for his great love wherewith he loved us.*
>
> (Ephesians 2:2–4 (italics added))

> [13]For, brethren, ye have been called unto liberty; only use not liberty for an occasion to the flesh, but by love serve one another. *[14]For all the law is fulfilled in one word, even in this; Thou shalt love thy neighbour as thyself. [15]But if ye bite and devour one another, take heed that ye be not consumed one of another.* [16]This I say then, *Walk in the Spirit, and ye shall not fulfill the lust of the flesh.* [17]For the *flesh lusteth against the Spirit,* and the Spirit against the flesh: and these *are contrary the one to the other:* so that ye cannot do the things that ye would. [18]But if ye be led of the Spirit, ye are not under the law. [19]Now the works of the flesh are manifest, which are these; Adultery, fornication, uncleanness, lasciviousness, [20]Idolatry, witchcraft, hatred, variance, emulations, wrath, strife, seditions, heresies, [21]Envyings, murders, drunkenness, revellings, and such like: of the which I tell you before, as I have also told you in time past, that they which do such things shall not inherit the kingdom of God. [22]But *the fruit of the Spirit is love, joy, peace, longsuffering, gentleness, goodness, faith, [23]Meekness, temperance: against such there is no law.* [24]And they that are Christ's have crucified the flesh with the affections and lusts. *[25]If we live in the Spirit, let us also walk in the Spirit.*
>
> (Galatians 5:13–25 (italics added))

We can try to fix it ourselves, but we will do nothing but make the situation worse, and prolong it. It ultimately gains nothing. If anything, we are to pray for those who are treating us wrong; bless them. Take them to our Lord and Savior. In our prayers, we are to let God know we realize they are His children (those who are doing us wrong) and we need Him to deal with them according to His—not our—Word. He was clear when He said *vengeance is mine saith the Lord.*

> *[18]If it be possible, as much as lieth in you, live peaceably with all men.* [19]Dearly beloved, *avenge not yourselves,* but rather give place unto wrath: for it is written, Vengeance is mine; I will repay, saith the Lord. [20]Therefore *if thine enemy hunger, feed him; if he thirst, give him drink: for in so doing thou shalt heap coals of fire on his head.*
>
> (Romans 12:18–20 (italics added))

As my youngest son would say, "He's (God's) got this." He will repay, which means it is not for us to fix or repay. He does not need our help in *repaying.* If we meddle in God's business, we have to make sure we do not end up reaping the negative as a result. He said *you will reap what you sow,* so let God handle it.

> [6]Let him that is taught in the word communicate unto him that teacheth in all good things.[7]Be not deceived; God is not mocked: for *whatsoever a man soweth, that shall he also reap. [8]For he that soweth to his flesh shall of the flesh reap corruption;* but he that soweth to the Spirit shall of the Spirit reap life everlasting.
>
> (Galatians 6:6-8 (italics added))

Sometimes, God needs to move people and situations out of our lives, because they are hindering the work of God concerning us. No matter what comes our way, stay in forgiveness. If we do not know what to pray, pray, *"Our Father, which art . . . ."*

6But thou, when thou prayest, enter into thy closet, and when thou hast shut thy door, pray to thy Father which is in secret; and thy Father which seeth in secret shall reward thee openly. 7But when ye pray, use not vain repetitions, as the heathen do: for they think that they shall be heard for their much speaking. 8Be not ye therefore like unto them: for your Father knoweth what things ye have need of, before ye ask him. 9After this manner therefore pray ye: Our Father which art in heaven, Hallowed be thy name. 10Thy kingdom come, Thy will be done in earth, as it is in heaven. 11Give us this day our daily bread. 12And forgive us our debts, as we forgive our debtors. 13And lead us not into temptation, but deliver us from evil: For thine is the kingdom, and the power, and the glory, for ever. Amen. 14For if ye forgive men their trespasses, your heavenly Father will also forgive you: 15But if ye forgive not men their trespasses, neither will your Father forgive your trespasses. 16Moreover when ye fast, be not, as the hypocrites, of a sad countenance: for they disfigure their faces, that they may appear unto men to fast. Verily I say unto you, They have their reward. 17But thou, when thou fastest, anoint thine head, and wash thy face; 18That thou appear not unto men to fast, but unto thy Father which is in secret: and thy Father, which seeth in secret, shall reward thee openly. 19Lay not up for yourselves treasures upon earth, where moth and rust doth corrupt, and where thieves break through and steal: 20But lay up for yourselves treasures in heaven, where neither moth nor rust doth corrupt, and where thieves do not break through nor steal: 21For where your treasure is, there will your heart be also.

(Matthew 6:6–21)

Yes, it is sometimes difficult to accept what God allows, but know without a doubt He will work every situation *out for our good.* Not for our bad, He wants us *to prosper and be in health even as our souls prosper.* We should make sure we are not too quick in saying there is no way this is God. What if it is God? Our best bet is to release the situation to God, especially if it concerns someone we dearly love. Additionally, let God deal all the way with the individual and allow Him to reconcile, if and only if, He sees fit.

> [27]But I say unto you which hear, *Love your enemies, do good to them which hate you,* [28]*Bless them that curse you, and pray for them which despitefully use you.* [29]And unto him that smiteth thee on the one cheek offer also the other; and him that taketh away thy cloak forbid not to take thy coat also.
>
> (Luke 6:27–29 (italics added))

CHAPTER 10

The Words You Speak

A good preventative measure is to ask God to not allow us to become *accountable* for our loved one's actions (to not hold it to our charge). Every idle *word and deed,* He said.

> [35]A good man out of the good treasure of the heart bringeth forth good things: and an evil man out of the evil treasure bringeth forth evil things. [36]But I say unto you, *That every idle word that men shall speak, they shall give account thereof in the day of judgment.* [37]For by thy words thou shalt be justified, and by thy words thou shalt be condemned.
>
> (Matthew 12:35–37 (italics added))

Just stand! When we know not what to do in life's trials, stand holding our critical position in battle. At the end of the day, we are to remember this day *is the day* God has made, and we are to remain *thankful unto Him and bless His name.*

> [17]I shall not die, but live, and declare the works of the LORD. [18]*The LORD* hath chastened me sore: but he hath not given me over unto death. [19]Open to me the gates of righteousness: I will go into them, and I will praise the LORD: [20]This gate of the LORD, into which the righteous shall enter. [21]*I will praise thee: for thou hast heard me, and art become my salvation.* [22]The stone which the builders refused is become the head stone of the corner.

> *²³This is the LORD's doing;* it is marvellous in our eyes. *²⁴This is the day which the LORD* hath made; we will rejoice and be glad in it. ²⁵Save now, I beseech thee, O LORD: O LORD, I beseech thee, send now prosperity. ²⁶Blessed be he that cometh in the name of the LORD: we have blessed you out of the house of the LORD. ²⁷God is the LORD, which hath shewed us light: bind the sacrifice with cords, even unto the horns of the altar. ²⁸Thou art my God, and I will praise thee: thou art my God, I will exalt thee. *²⁹O give thanks unto the LORD; for he is good: for his mercy endureth for ever*
> (Psalm 118:17–29 (italics added))

We may not understand why, but He is still good!

> ¹Make a joyful noise unto the LORD, all ye lands. ²Serve the LORD with gladness: come before his presence with singing. *³Know ye that the LORD he is God:* it is he that hath made us, and not we ourselves; we are his people, and the sheep of his pasture. ⁴Enter into his gates with thanksgiving, and into his courts with praise: be thankful unto him, and bless his name. *⁵For the LORD is good; his mercy is everlasting; and his truth endureth to all generations.*
> (Psalm 100: 1–5 (italics added))

We are to accept what God allows and at the same time, build up our most Holy faith. Stay where God can continually forgive us. People in alt and unforgiveness "bite off more than they can chew." When it shows up in sickness, they need to reflect on where they grasped the situation and buried it in their heart. The heart pumps the blood throughout the body. When it becomes unclean, impurity will fester and flow throughout the body in some format.

At the end of the day, we are to ask God to cover us and to hide us (see Psalm 91). He has a *secret place* where He can protect us and *hide us* from all the *wiles of the devil* and keep us, so nothing *will harm us.* Victory is ours, and we have the power to walk on and over the adversary's attempts.

[10]Finally, my brethren, be strong in the Lord, and in the power of his might. [11]Put on the whole armour of God, that ye may be able to stand against the wiles of the devil. [12]For *we wrestle not against flesh and blood, but against principalities, against powers, against the rulers of the darkness of this world, against spiritual wickedness in high places.*

(Ephesians 6:10–12 (italics added))

[18]And he said unto them, I beheld Satan as lightning fall from heaven. [19]*Behold, I give unto you power to tread on serpents and scorpions, and over all the power of the enemy: and nothing shall by any means hurt you.* [20]Notwithstanding in this rejoice not, that the spirits are subject unto you; but rather rejoice, because your names are written in heaven.

(Luke 10:18–20 (italics added))

God is *our fortress;* He is our *help in* the time of *trouble.*

[1]God is our refuge and strength, a *very present help in trouble.* [2]Therefore will not we fear, though the earth be removed, and though the mountains be carried into the midst of the sea; [3]Though the waters thereof roar and be troubled, though the mountains shake with the swelling thereof. Selah.

(Psalm 46:1–3 (italics added))

In Romans 4:17–21 (italics added), we are commanded to call those things which are not as though they were:

[17](As it is written, I have made thee a father of many nations,) before him whom he believed, even God, who quickeneth the dead, and calleth those things which be not as though they were.[18]Who against hope believed in hope, that he might become the father of many nations, according to that which was spoken, So shall thy seed be. [19]And being not weak in faith, he considered not his own body now dead, when he was about an hundred years old, neither yet the deadness of Sarah's womb: [20]*He staggered not at the promise of God through unbelief; but was strong*

in faith, giving glory to God; [21]And being fully persuaded that, what he had promised, he was able also to perform.

God is more than aware we are going to face problems.

> [1]Man that *is born of a woman is of few days and full of trouble.* [2]He cometh forth like a flower, and is cut down: he fleeth also as a shadow, and continueth not.[3]And doth thou open thine eyes upon such an one, and bringest me into judgment with thee?
> (Job 14:1–3 (italics added))

Man born of woman will have problems. He already took care of all of our problems, when he overcame the world.

> [31]Jesus answered them, *Do ye now believe?* [32]Behold, the hour cometh, yea, is now come, that ye shall be scattered, every man to his own, and shall leave me alone: and yet I am not alone, because the Father is with me.[33] These things I have spoken unto you, that in me ye might have peace. In the world *ye shall have tribulation: but be of good cheer; I have overcome the world.*
> (John 16:31–33 (italics added))

Whatever our situation, we must remember we *are* more than a conqueror through Christ, and we *can do all things* through Him. His Word says it in Philippians 4:12–13 (italics added):

> [12]I know both how to be abased, and I know how to abound: every where and in all things I am instructed both to be full and to be hungry, both to abound and to suffer need. [13]I can do all things through Christ which strengtheneth me.

We must have faith; we must stand in faith, in order to procure the victory. We have to believe God can and will do anything. As long as our prayers line up with His Word and with what it proclaims, we can count on it. The bottom line is nothing coming against us is going to win.

[16]Behold, I have created the smith that bloweth the coals in the fire, and that bringeth forth an instrument for his work; and I have created the waster to destroy. [17]*No weapon that is formed against thee shall prosper; and every tongue that shall rise against thee in judgment thou shalt condemn.* This is the *heritage of the servants of the* LORD, and their righteousness is of me, saith the LORD.

(Isaiah 54:16–17 (italics added))

Every evil plot shaped to attack, He has proclaimed it is not going to prosper. He is counting on us though to do our part. He said we are to condemn it! God is not and can not go against His Word. We are to take every word spoken and condemn them! We can not expect Him to do it, we must do it. If we are His, it is our right, it is our heritage. We must realize how powerful our words are.

[62]What and if ye shall see the Son of man ascend up where he was before? [63]It is the *spirit that quickeneth; the flesh profiteth nothing: the words that I speak unto you, they are spirit, and they are life.* [64]But there are some of you that believe not. For Jesus knew from the beginning who they were that believed not, and who should betray him.

(John 6:62–64 italics added))

A strong example of how our words are spirit and life is illustrated through the woman with the issue of blood.

[16]No man putteth a piece of new cloth unto an old garment, for that which is put in to fill it up taketh from the garment, and the rent is made worse. [17]Neither do men put new wine into old bottles: else the bottles break, and the wine runneth out, and the bottles perish: but they put new wine into new bottles, and both are preserved. [18]While he spake these things unto them, behold, there came a certain ruler, and worshipped him, saying, My daughter is even now dead: but come and lay thy hand upon her, and she shall live. [19]And Jesus arose, and followed him, and so did his disciples. [20]And, behold, a woman,

which was diseased with an issue of blood twelve years, came behind him, and touched the hem of his garment: [21]For she said within herself, If I may but touch his garment, I shall be whole. [22]But Jesus turned him about, and when he saw her, he said, Daughter, be of good comfort; thy faith hath made thee whole. And the woman was made whole from that hour.

(Matthew 9:16–22 (italics added))

He did not touch her; she touched Him. Please recognize the words she spoke were mixed with faith. It was her faith, but God was faithful unto her. We must have faith in God. Another strong example of God's Word proving itself is the story of Jehosaphat. Jehosaphat had situation after situation come his way, but he maintained his faith.

CHAPTER 11

God Will Handle Your Enemy

When we are having problems, just like with the example we had through the children of Israel, we are to cry out to our Lord and Savior, and He will help us. But first, we must establish we are His, we are an heir.

⁸So then they that are in the flesh cannot please God. ⁹But ye are not in the flesh, but in the Spirit, if so be that the Spirit of God dwell in you. Now *if any man have not the Spirit of Christ, he is none of his.* ¹⁰And if Christ be in you, the body is dead because of sin; but the Spirit is life because of righteousness. ¹¹But if *the Spirit of him that raised up Jesus from the dead dwell in you,* he that raised up Christ from the dead *shall also quicken your mortal bodies by his Spirit that dwelleth in you.* ¹²Therefore, brethren, we are debtors, not to the flesh, to live after the flesh. ¹³For if ye live after the flesh, ye shall die: but if ye through the Spirit do mortify the deeds of the body, ye shall live. ¹⁴*For as many as are led by the Spirit of God, they are the sons of God.* ¹⁵For ye have not received the spirit of bondage again to fear; *but ye have received the Spirit of adoption, whereby we cry, Abba, Father.* ¹⁶The *Spirit itself beareth witness with our spirit,* that we are the children of God: ¹⁷*And if children, then heirs; heirs of God, and joint-heirs with Christ; if so be that we suffer with him, that we may be also glorified together.* ¹⁸For I reckon that the *sufferings of this present time are not worthy to be compared with the glory which shall be revealed in us.* ¹⁹For the

earnest expectation of the creature waiteth for the *manifestation of the sons of God.*

(Romans 8:8–19 (italics added))

The next few pages will predominately focus on II Chronicles 20:5–25 (italics added), as these verses are the perfect example of the enemy not prevailing over God's people/children:

> ⁵And Jehoshaphat stood in the congregation of Judah and Jerusalem, in the house of the LORD, before the new court, ⁶And said, O LORD God of our fathers, art not thou God in heaven? and *rulest not thou over all the kingdoms of the heathen? and in thine hand is there not power and might, so that none is able to withstand thee?* ⁷Art not thou our God, who didst drive out the inhabitants of this land before thy people Israel, *and gavest it to the seed of Abraham thy friend for ever?* ⁸And they dwelt therein, and have built thee a sanctuary therein for thy name, saying, ⁹*If, when evil cometh upon us, as the sword, judgment, or pestilence, or famine, we stand before this house, and in thy presence, (for thy name is in this house,) and cry unto thee in our affliction, then thou wilt hear and help.* ¹⁰And now, behold, the children of Ammon and Moab and mount Seir, whom thou wouldest not let Israel invade, when they came out of the land of Egypt, but *they turned from them, and destroyed them not;* ¹¹Behold, I say, how they reward us, to come to cast us out of thy possession, which thou hast given us to inherit. ¹²*O our God, wilt thou not judge them? for we have no might against this great company that cometh against us;* neither know we *what to do:* but *our eyes are upon thee.*

Jephosaphat recognized he needed God, but he also had faith God was watching.

> ¹³ And all *Judah stood before the LORD,* with their little ones, their wives, and their children.

You have not forgotten Judah is interpreted to mean praise have you?

> ¹⁴Then upon Jahaziel the son of Zechariah, the son of Benaiah, the son of Jeiel, the son of Mattaniah, a Levite of the sons of Asaph, *came the Spirit of the LORD in the midst of the congregation;* ¹⁵And he said, *Hearken ye, all Judah, and ye inhabitants of Jerusalem, and thou king Jehoshaphat, Thus saith the LORD unto you, Be not afraid nor dismayed by reason of this great multitude; for the battle is not yours, but God's.*

So God sent His servant Jahaziel to speak to His people, telling them not to fear the enemy. (Do not forget there is a great multitude against them.) Not only are they commanded not to fear, but they are also informed the battle belongs to God. Notice Jehoshaphat did not run to his Mom and Dad or his buddies for advice. He took instruction from God. We must watch who we let feed into our spirit.

> ¹⁶ *To morrow go ye down against them:* behold, they come up by the cliff of Ziz; and ye shall *find them at the end of the brook,* before the wilderness of Jeruel. ¹⁷*Ye shall not need to fight in this battle: set yourselves, stand ye still, and see the salvation of the LORD with you, O Judah and Jerusalem: fear not, nor be dismayed; to morrow go out against them: for the LORD will be with you.*

Not only are Judah and Jerusalem told not to fear the enemy, they are told to not run from or to do it their way. They were specifically instructed to not fight, and to set/place themselves against the enemy. Next, they were told to stand still. Remember from earlier, stand in a military sense means *to hold your critical position in battle.* We can equate it to *marking time,* ready and waiting to take our next set of directions at a moment's notice. By no means does it indicate lay down on the job and get comfortable; it means get ready to receive orders.

> ¹⁸And Jehoshaphat *bowed his head with his face to the ground:* and *all Judah and the inhabitants of Jerusalem fell before the* LORD, *worshipping the* LORD. ¹⁹And the Levites, of the children of the Kohathites, and of the children of the Korhites, *stood up to praise the* LORD *God of Israel with a loud voice on high.*

Jehoshaphat and the people of God started worshiping the Lord with a loud voice. When we are in battle, it is not time to go sit in a corner. It is time to show God we have the faith to believe He is and will do what His Word says He will do. Additionally, I want to point out the people of God got on one accord; they fell before God in worship and praised God with a loud voice. They recognized God was in control; His hand was over their situation.

> ²⁰*And they rose early in the morning, and went forth into the wilderness* of Tekoa: and as they went forth, *Jehoshaphat stood and said, Hear me, O Judah, and ye inhabitants of Jerusalem; Believe in the* LORD *your God, so shall ye be established; believe his prophets, so shall ye prosper.*

Jehoshaphat reiterated they were to believe God and the Word which came forth to them. Another scripture which supports Jehoshaphat's message to the people is found in Isaiah 54:13–15 (italics added):

> ¹³And all thy children shall be taught of the LORD; and great shall be the peace of thy children. *¹⁴In righteousness shalt thou be established: thou shalt be far from oppression;* for thou shalt not fear: and from terror; for it shall not come near thee. ¹⁵Behold, they shall surely gather together, but not by me: *whosoever shall gather together against thee shall fall for thy sake.*

No one is saying everything is going to appear easy, but we are to have faith in God. Always count on the fact He is with us. He always has, and He will repeatedly fight and continue to come through for us—always. As proclaimed in Exodus 17:15, ". . . the *Lord is our banner.*" We just can not lose focus on where our help comes; He is faithful. He said it like this in Hebrews 13:4–6 (italics added):

> [4]Marriage is honourable in all, and the bed undefiled: but whoremongers and adulterers God will judge. [5]Let your conversation be without covetousness; and *be content with such things as ye have*: for he hath said, *I will never leave thee, nor forsake thee.* [6]So that we may *boldly say, The Lord is my helper, and I will not fear what man shall do unto me.*

God will come through for us in His time; not our time, but He always comes through. He is our help. If we need to know how and when He is going to do it, He is more than capable of letting us know. Let Him fight the battle. We need to just do our part on what He instructs us to do, and stay out the flesh trying to fix it. No matter what, just like with Jehoshaphat, keep praising God. It is not wait until the battle is over before we praise Him, praise Him always (especially when we get in the heat of the battle). Continue to believe the victory is coming; the victory is on the way.

> [21]And when he had consulted with the people, *he appointed singers unto the Lord, and that should praise the beauty of holiness, as they went out before the army, and to say, Praise the Lord; for his mercy endureth for ever.* [22]And *when they began to sing and to praise, the Lord set ambushments against the children of Ammon, Moab, and mount Seir, which were come against Judah; and they were smitten.*

This is the best example I can share for us to praise God when we are going through our roughest times.

> [23]For the children of Ammon and Moab stood up against the inhabitants of mount Seir, utterly to slay and destroy them: and *when they had made an end of the inhabitants of Seir, every one helped to destroy another.*

This situation indicates, the enemy turned on himself. What better way to ensure defeat. Once again, we are more than a conqueror.

> [24]*And when Judah came toward the watch tower in the wilderness, they looked unto the multitude, and, behold, they were dead bodies fallen to the earth, and none escaped.*

People may appear to get by for a time, but . . . He said to touch not. 1 Chronicles 16:21–23 (italics added) reads:

> [21]He suffered no man to do them wrong: yea, he reproved kings for their sakes,[22]Saying, *Touch not mine anointed, and do my prophets no harm. [23]Sing unto the LORD, all the earth; shew forth from day to day his salvation.*

After the battle, they proclaimed victory over the enemy and laid claim to the enemy's goods.

> [25]And when Jehoshaphat and *his people came to take away the spoil of them, they found among them in abundance both riches with the dead bodies, and precious jewels, which they stripped off for themselves,* more than they could carry away: and they were *three days in gathering of the spoil, it was so much.*

Remember, we are instructed to keep the faith and know God will see us through. We must continue to believe, it does not matter the situation, God can handle it. Just set ourselves in position, and stand as He fights the battle. We will see the victory. Our faith has to super cede every situation and condition. God will repay His enemies.

> [18]*According to their deeds, accordingly he will repay, fury to his adversaries, recompence to his enemies; to the islands he will repay recompence.* [19]So shall they fear the name of the LORD from the west, and his glory from the rising of the sun. *When the enemy shall come in like a flood, the Spirit of the LORD shall lift up a standard against him.* [20]And

the Redeemer shall come to Zion, and unto them that turn from transgression in Jacob, saith the LORD.

(Isaiah 59:18–20 (italics added))

We are to keep our minds stayed on Jesus; He will give us peace. Not just peace, but He will give us perfect peace.

3 Thou wilt keep *him in perfect peace,* whose mind is stayed on thee: *because he trusteth in thee.* *4Trust ye in the LORD for ever:* for in the LORD JEHOVAH is everlasting strength: 5For *he bringeth down them that dwell on high;* the lofty city, he layeth it low; he layeth it low, even to the ground; he bringeth it even to the dust.

(Isaiah 26:3–5 (italics added))

It is time to move forward at His and only at His command. We are to make sure we are moving at His command and listening and gleaning wisdom from Him. Ask Him to give an added bonus of orchestrating and coordinating the day. He will lead and guide us, if we just ask Him. There is an excellent scripture which states whatever condition we are in to make sure we are *content.*

11Not that I speak in respect of want: for I have learned, in whatsoever state I am, therewith to be content.

(Philippians 4:11)

Expect bigger and better from God. We are enduring hardness as a good soldier, for a reason. In due season, we will reap if we faint not.

2And the things that thou hast heard of me among many witnesses, the same commit thou to faithful men, who shall be able to teach others also. *3Thou therefore endure hardness, as a good soldier of Jesus Christ.* 4No man that warreth entangleth himself with the affairs of this life; that he may please him who hath chosen him to be a soldier.

(II Timothy 2:2–4 (italics added))

[8]For he that soweth to his flesh shall of the flesh reap corruption; but he that soweth to the Spirit shall of the Spirit reap life everlasting. [9]*And let us not be weary in well doing: for in due season we shall reap, if we faint not.* [10]*As we have therefore opportunity, let us do good unto all men,* especially unto them who are of the household of faith.

(Galatians 6:8–10 (italics added))

CHAPTER 12

Great is Our God

It is your season! Prepare for it, dress like it, and act like it. Get ready to receive your harvest. He said we are going to reap if we do not faint. This is not to say go buy a new wardrobe; it is saying out of what we have, we are to present ourselves a living sacrifice. Are we *acceptable,* or can everyone tell we are going through a hard time because it is written all over our demeanor?

> [1]I beseech you therefore, brethren, by the mercies of God, that ye *present your bodies a living sacrifice, holy, acceptable unto God, which is your reasonable service.* [2]And be not conformed to this world: but *be ye transformed by the renewing of your mind, that ye may prove what is that good, and acceptable, and perfect, will of God.* [3]For I say, through the grace given unto me, to every man that is among you, not to think of himself more highly than he ought to think; but to think soberly, according as God *hath dealt to every man the measure of faith.*
>
> (Romans 12:1–3 (italics added))

Gird up our loins; we are children of God!

> [12]Unto whom it was revealed, that not unto themselves, but unto us they did minister the things, which are now reported unto you by them that have preached the gospel unto you with the Holy Ghost sent down from heaven; which things

the angels desire to look into. *¹³Wherefore gird up the loins of your mind, be sober, and hope to the end for the grace that is to be brought unto you at the revelation of Jesus Christ;* ¹⁴As obedient children, not fashioning yourselves according to the former lusts in your ignorance.

(1 Peter 1:12–14 (italics added))

Count our blessings. If we do not think our storm could have been worse, all we have to do is visit the local hospital or morgue. We are still in the land of the living and as such are to press toward the mark of the prize. His Word tells us our response we are to give when He said, *"Be thankful unto Him and bless His name for the Lord is good His mercy is everlasting and His truth endureth to all generations* (Psalm 100:4–5 (italics added))." Great is our reward.

¹¹Blessed are ye, *when men shall revile you, and persecute you, and shall say all manner of evil against you falsely, for my sake.* ¹²Rejoice, and *be exceeding glad: for great is your reward in heaven:* for so persecuted they the prophets which were before you. ¹³Ye are the salt of the earth: but if the salt have lost his savour, wherewith shall it be salted? it is thenceforth good for nothing, but to be cast out, and to be trodden under foot of men.

(Matthew 5:11–13 (italics added))

How can we *bless His name* if all we are doing is repeatedly becoming consumed by past hurts and poor decisions others have made concerning us. Are we enduring negativity due to the way we are handling the storms of life? Are we out of alignment? Think about your car when it is out of alignment; not only are you pulling the wrong direction, you have to fight for a straight path. Additionally, it wears on your tires and makes your journey bumpy.

It is really difficult to bless His name and simultaneously run people down for the negative they have done to us. Give it to God;

cast your care, and do not take it back. We all should make sure others are not trying to unnecessarily discuss the situation with us. Sometimes, individuals (especially friends and family) want to keep bringing things up to us. All it does is keep our hurt fresh, and it does not allow for healing to take place. He said to endure hardness, but He did not say any part of it was to keep rehashing the past. It is hard to keep our eyes *on things above* and keep them on things behind (our past) at the same time.

> ²*Set your affection on things above, not on things on the earth.* ³For ye are dead, and your life is hid with Christ in God.
>
> (Colossians 3:2 (italics added))

It is either one or the other. No one is saying we are never allowed to discuss matters with others. I am just saying make sure we are wise about it and only on an as–needed basis. Again, whatever we do, we can not let conversations draw us out of forgiveness. If we have an alt against our brother, before we go into prayer, we are ordained to get it right. How can we say *we love God whom* we have *never seen,* but we have an issue with our neighbor or brother.

> ¹⁹We love him, because he first loved us. ²⁰*If a man say, I love God, and hateth his brother, he is a liar:* for he that *loveth not his brother whom he hath seen,* how can he *love God whom he hath not seen?* ²¹And this *commandment have we from him, That he who loveth God love his brother also.*
>
> (1 John 4:19–21 (italics added))

Something is wrong somewhere, and it is not with God. Ask Him to reveal areas of concern. Seriously seek Him so you remain in *right standing with Him* (the Kingdom of God – righteous).

Who are we asking to help in our storm? Who is the prayer partner? Ask God about them, to reveal what we are to say and not to say to them, first. The purpose of a prayer partner is to take our situation to God, to intercede for us. But please trust and believe the veil was already rent, so we can also go to God for ourselves. Do we need to spend time praying for ourselves? He also said we are to *trust no man.*

> [2]While I live will I praise the LORD: I will sing praises unto my God while I have any being. [3]*Put not your trust in princes, nor in the son of man, in whom there is no help.*
>
> (Psalm 146:2–4 (italics added))

This is simply to say anyone can become a tool of the adversary at any given time. (Remember the fruit.) We have been advised to pray without ceasing. How is that possible? We are to stay in a condition where we can connect with God at any time we need Him. Listening to the Word, songs, and reading our Bible are a few ways which will assist. It is hard to do, when we are doing things which are not *pleasing to God.* If all God needs is a willing vessel, what do you think the adversary needs? Know who is doing the leading. Remember, if someone is off by just a simple degree when they plot their journey, they can totally miss their destination. Are we His sheep? If so, we will not follow the stranger's voice.

Eventually, the day will come as we continue *to seek God and His righteousness,* our circle of friends may become smaller and smaller. As we grow in God, we will discuss matters with others less and less. He wants to *add unto us* (Matthew 6). We have to get to a point we move past certain traps real quick. When we see ourselves being drawn into conversations with the wrong motive, we will now recognize how important it is to stay in forgiveness. Things will not continue to consume/weigh us, and we will more quickly move from old thoughts. People may tell us they do not understand how we can let someone off the hook for what they did to us. He said, *My ways are not your ways, and My thoughts are not your thoughts.*

> [7]Let the *wicked forsake his way,* and the unrighteous man his thoughts: and *let him return unto the LORD, and he will have mercy upon him;* and to our God, for *he will abundantly pardon.* [8]*For my thoughts are not your thoughts, neither are your ways my ways, saith the LORD.* [9]For as the heavens are higher than the earth, *so are my ways higher than your ways, and my thoughts than your thoughts.*
>
> (Isaiah 55:7–9 (italics added))

Well they are not you, and what are their motives? Some people are just messy. Do not fall for it; recognize when individuals are simply tools of the adversary who want to resurrect old stuff. Only the devil is the *accuser of the brethren,* and those whom he uses display the same fruit. If they only knew what we now know, they too would quickly release a person from offenses, so they could minimize their own storm. God's command to the storm is this, *"Peace be still."* He did not engage in conversation with the storm, He took control and commanded it. He *cares* when we are on the verge of *perishing.* This is why He will harness our storms.

> [37]And there arose a great storm of wind, and the waves beat into the ship, so that it was now full. [38]And he was in the hinder part of the ship, asleep on a pillow: and they awake him, and say unto him, Master, carest thou not that we perish? [39]And he arose, and rebuked the wind, and said unto the sea, *Peace, be still. And the wind ceased, and there was a great calm.*
>
> (Mark 4:37–39 (italics added))

Our temptations are not new.

> [12]Wherefore let him that thinketh he standeth *take heed lest he fall.* [13]*There hath no temptation taken you but such as is common to man: but God is faithful, who will not suffer you to be tempted above that ye are able; but will with the temptation also make a way to escape,* that

ye may be able to bear it. [14]Wherefore, my dearly beloved, flee from idolatry.

> (1 Corinthians 10:12–14 (italics added))

The last part of these scriptures tells us to *flee idolatry*; remember He is a jealous God, and we are *not* to love anyone or thing more than we love Him.

Are we asking how long Lord? Just remember, He promised He will provide a way of escape. At the end of the day, our desire is to remain in a position to have Him say the following:

> [21]His lord said unto him, *Well done, thou good and faithful servant: thou hast been faithful over a few things, I will make thee ruler over many things: enter thou into the joy of thy lord.*
>
> (Matthew 20:21 (italics added))

Amen!

About the Author

Dr. Tammara S. Grays is first and foremost an educator. She has taught middle and high school levels (also, the college level) in Ohio for more than twenty years, where she resides with her family. She has been a consultant and coach for the past seven years. Additionally, her gifting is the office of a teacher.

Dr. Grays has been an active member in the ministry for more than twenty-five years. As such, she is a firm believer of God's Word. *The Father Knows Best* is Dr. Grays's first published work.

If you would like to reach Dr. Grays concerning conferences or seminars, you may contact her via the following:

dr.tsgrays@gmail.com